Continuing praise for Louis Evely's spiritual writing:

"In *Suffering*, Evely expounds the age-old challenge of the problem of evil, and in clear language and equally clear logic explains suffering, its sacredness, its redemptive value.

Evely proclaims no new doctrine but he gives old doctrines a value and meaning that all too seldom are brought to light. Though its theme is suffering, the book is in no sense depressing. The author stresses God's love for man and God's need to express that love in a way that man cannot fail to comprehend. . . . The series of meditations [at the end of the book] . . . climax a volume that could be of great value alike to priest, religious and layman." *America*

". . . a profoundly religious book. . . . Those who suffer share the feelings of God, share His way of seeing the world. But Evely despises Pharisaism, and those who make a fetish of pain will find no sympathy in him. . . . The true mystic in love with life and enamored of joy will readily grant that Evely is a writer of classics." *Eternity*

"If you think no one can have anything new or readable or meditateable to say about suffering, try Louis Evely. He writes about this most personal and painful facet of Christianity from the inside, and creates, instead of the traditional apology for suffering, a climate of love where suffering exists because vulnerability exists, and because God gives to the point of giving a nature like His own. . . . The book concludes with sixteen meditations, beautiful Evely exercises in meeting God where He is." *Eucharist*

". . . a solid, practical, and thoroughly modern work of meditation, endowed with all of the qualities that have made Evely today's most widely read spiritual writer." *Virginia Kirkus Service*

SUFFERING

LOUIS EVELY

TRANSLATED BY
MARIE-CLAUDE THOMPSON

IMAGE BOOKS
A DIVISION OF DOUBLEDAY & COMPANY, INC.
GARDEN CITY, NEW YORK

Image Books edition by special arrangement with
Seabury Press
Image Books edition published September 1974

Original edition: *Souffrance,*
published by the author.

Nihil obstat: Thomas J. Beary, Censor Librorum
Imprimatur: ✠ Robert F. Joyce, Bishop of Burlington
October 24, 1966

CONTENTS

There is at this moment, in the world, at the back of some forsaken church, or even in an ordinary house, or at the turning of a deserted path, a poor man who joins his hands and from the depth of his misery, without very well knowing what he is saying, or without saying anything, thanks the good Lord for having made him free, for having made him capable of loving. There is somewhere else, I do not know where, a mother who hides her face for the last time in the hollow of a little breast which will beat no more, a mother next to her dead child who offers to God the groan of an exhausted resignation, as if the Voice which has thrown the suns into space as a hand throws grain, the Voice which makes the worlds tremble, had just murmured gently into her ear, "Pardon me. One day you will know, you will understand, you will give me thanks. But now, what I am looking for from you is your pardon. Pardon." These—this harassed woman, this poor man—are at the heart of the mystery, at the heart of the universal creation and in the very secret of God. What can I say of it? Language is at the service of the intelligence. And what these people have understood, they have understood by a faculty superior to the intelligence although not in the least in contradiction with it—or rather, by a profound and irresistible movement of the soul which engaged all the faculties at once, which engaged to the depth their entire nature . . . Yes, at the moment that this man, this woman, accepted their destiny, accepted themselves, humbly—the mystery of the creation was being accomplished in them. While they were thus, without knowing it, running the entire risk of their human conduct, they were realizing themselves fully in the charity of Christ, becoming themselves, according to the words of St. Paul, other Christs. In short, they were saints.

Georges Bernanos

SUFFERING

I

SUFFERING

The meaning of evil, the meaning of suffering, is what Christ himself invites us to meditate on after the paschal event.

"O foolish men," he then said to them, "and slow of heart to believe all that the prophets have spoken!" (Lk. 24, 25). He means us. Few characters of the Gospel are as much like us as these disappointed, overburdened men who were walking along without joy and without hope, and who for hours had to have the passion explained to them by a companion until they finally came to believe in the resurrection.

After every trial, after every cross, we walk again along this road of despair, the road where the pilgrims of Emmaus journeyed, sadness clouding their faces, conversing and discussing, broken, disillusioned, annihilated. ". . . Jesus himself drew near and went with them. But their eyes were kept from recognizing him" (Lk. 24, 16).

And they complain, to him, about himself: "We had hoped . . . we thought he would redeem us . . . and he has been killed, crucified. Angels say indeed that he is alive, the tomb was seen empty. But for him, he has not been seen."

And then comes the affectionate rebuke: "O foolish men! . . . *Was it not necessary that the Christ should suffer these things and enter into his glory?* —And beginning with Moses and all the prophets, he interpreted to them in all the Scriptures the things concerning himself."

*

This conversation, this meditation during which the Lord, through the understanding of the Scriptures, explained to

them how the suffering of Christ—which had become theirs
—was necessary, good, efficacious . . . we too must try to hear
it. This very path, we too must take it again with the Lord,
in the light of the Scriptures.

Suffering, disappointment, crucifixion—we should not resign ourselves to them. We must, in our turn, find their divine, triumphal meaning "in the prophets." What concerned
Christ is also what concerns us. For we and he are but one
since our baptism. Each of us is incorporated into him forever.

There is only one means to endure our suffering, and that
is to understand his, to hook ours onto his, to remember that
ours *is* his. "I am glorified in them" (Jn. 17, 10), but also:
"in my flesh I complete what is lacking in Christ's afflictions
for the sake of his body, that is, the Church" (Col. 1, 24).

"Beginning with Moses . . ." Like the Church, we will go
back even to the first sacrifice, the sacrifice of "Abel, the just,"
recalled every day in the Canon of the Mass.

This comes shortly after the consecration: "And this do
you deign to regard with gracious and kindly attention and
hold acceptable, as you deigned to accept the offerings of
Abel, your just servant . . ."

*

Abel: the first man to be hurt through no fault of his
own, the first man who got into trouble without deserving it,
the first man whose inexplicable suffering atoned for the sin
of another. For Cain will be marked with a sign which will
protect him, and the New Testament insinuates that this sign
was Abel's blood.

"In the course of time Cain brought to the Lord an offering of the fruit of the ground, and Abel brought of the first-
lings of his flock, and of their fat portions. And the Lord had
regard for Abel and his offering, but for Cain and his offering
he had no regard. So Cain was very angry, and his countenance fell. The Lord said to Cain, 'Why are you angry, and
why has your countenance fallen? If you do well, will you not

be accepted? And if you do not do well, sin is couching at the door; its desire is for you, but you must master it.'

"Cain said to Abel his brother, 'Let us go out to the field.' And when they were in the field, Cain rose up against his brother Abel, and killed him" (Gen. 4, 3–8).

This narrative, like the story of Adam and Eve, like those of the tower of Babel and the Flood, is indeed the story of the original sin of man, of the fundamental refusal to love, to commit oneself, to trust, to prefer another, to forget one's will in favor of another's will.

If Jesus, the new Adam, made good the fault of the earthly paradise, it can be said also that he atoned for, compensated for, that he gave the counter-image of *Cain*: "For this is the message which you have heard from the beginning, that we should love one another, and not be like Cain who was of the evil one and murdered his brother" (1 Jn. 3, 11–12).

*

Adam sinned against the first commandment. Cain's sin is already a sin against the second commandment, which Jesus revealed to be like the first. ". . . whoever does not do right is not of God, nor he who does not love his brother" (1 Jn. 3, 10).

"Then the Lord said to Cain, 'Where is Abel your brother?' " This echoes "Adam, where are you?" Our repentance comes always from an initiative of God.

For each of our returns, for each of our confessions, let us cry out with joy: it is God who is calling us back to him, it is God who, already, is working within us, is raising us up to himself, is asking for our presence and our love.

"Cain answered . . ." coarsely at first. It is extraordinary how much he is like us, Cain! "I do not know. Am I my brother's keeper?"

But God goes on: "What have you done!", what a mess! God is afflicted. God, whose only joy is to bless, has to threaten, to scold, to punish.

Cain said to the Lord, "My punishment is greater than I can bear. Behold, thou hast driven me this day away from the ground; and from thy face I shall be hidden; and I shall be a fugitive and a wanderer on the earth. . . ." There is something touching in this sudden change. This can be seen among very primitive people, in the archaic stories of every civilization. Characters all of one piece, and who go, at once, to the extremes: it is great. It is also very awkward, a little childish.

Cain loves God—with a clumsy, blind, petty love, a foolish love, a jealous love. Cain thinks that he loves God, but he cannot stand the idea that God prefers someone else. He is a jealous man, mad with anger—an anger which is dreadfully culpable, but also, probably, terribly painful. Let us not hasten to be "the first to throw a stone" at him.

*

At all times there have been people to work out the motives of the incident. Why did God prefer Abel's sacrifice? Then, in order to save the traditional canons of justice, the following reason was invented: Cain offered rotten fruit, damaged vegetables, he cheated on the goods. Abel, on the contrary, offered the best of his flock. According to this line of thought, everything is explained. If Cain, like Abel, had sacrificed the best, chosen the most beautiful fruits and the first vegetables of the season, God, sensitive to these vegetable delicacies, God, fond of first fruits, would not have preferred Abel!

Now: at the very first words of the Lord, one can precisely see that the important thing is not what is offered, but the way it is offered.

What counts is not what one does, but how and why one does it. What is important is our acts more than our words, our motives more than our acts.

You are doing a "good deed"? This is *perhaps* agreeable to God: why are you doing it? In order to have a good conscience? Then it is for your pleasure that you do it and not for his. Because you love the beneficiary? This is more reassuring. The second commandment is like the first.

The important thing is the interior disposition. Only that reaches God which is done through love. To sacrifice something is to make it sacred, to make it God's, to make it love. All the rest is pretense. "I hate, I despise your feasts, and I take no delight in your solemn assemblies. Even though you offer me your burnt offerings and cereal offerings, I will not accept them, and the peace offerings of your fatted beasts I will not look upon them. Take away from me the noise of your songs. . . . But let justice roll down like waters, and righteousness like an everflowing stream" (Amos 5, 21–24). "Is not this the fast that I choose: to loose the bonds of wickedness, to undo the thongs of the yoke, to let the op-pressed go free, and to break every yoke? Is it not to share your bread with the hungry . . . ?" (Is. 58, 6–7). What God wants is an upright heart, somebody who loves him well, who loves him rightly.

*

"By faith Abel offered to God a more acceptable sacrifice than Cain, through which he received approval as righteous, God bearing witness by accepting his gifts; he died, but through his faith he is still speaking" (Heb. 11, 4).

In what way does Abel have more *faith* than Cain?

One can only grasp Abel's faith if one has understood the beatitudes. It is the theme of poverty which, once more, will give us the key to this divine affirmation.

God prefers—the poor. God prefers the younger son to the first-born, the sterile to the gratified, the unhappy to the sat-isfied, the children to the adults, the sinners to the "just."

Cain, the first-born, offered a first-born's sacrifice, a sacri-fice sure to be accepted, a sacrifice of the rich, of one who is well introduced; a sacrifice without the spirit of poverty; a sacrifice with guaranteed plenary indulgence. Cain was sure of his rights and his merits.

Abel offers as the younger son; he knows that he is some-body who does not count. "If God looks at my sacrifice, it will be because of *his* kindness, not because of my merits." This is Abel's prayer, his only assurance. Abel's sacrifice is an act of pure abandonment, of pure confidence, a naïvely gratuitous act.

Cain and Abel, they are already the Pharisee and the publican.

God's preference for the poor, in a way that is beyond the concept of what men have decided to call justice, can be found again and again throughout the history of the people of God. The story of Esau and Jacob is well known: it is not a question here of a punishment of greediness, even less of an encouragement to use cunning methods and to lie. But— in spite of sinful man's pitiful means—it is a matter of God granting to someone other than a "first-born" a favor and a blessing which he proudly thought only he was entitled to.

The same reversal takes place in favor of Ephraim (and in prejudice of Manasseh) by the hands of the dying Jacob. Jacob is far from being a saint in a stained-glass window: those who would have doubts about it have but to read Genesis 30, 25–43. The tricks found by Jacob to increase the standing of his flock are perhaps clever, certainly not edifying. But this old joker had improved with age. So much so that on his deathbed he comes to make an extraordinary gesture: Joseph brings to him two sons, and Jacob, crossing his hands, gives to Ephraim the blessing "which was the due" of Manasseh, putting the younger son "before" the first-born. Joseph protests, Joseph believes still, as for him, in rights, in legitimate privileges, in prerogatives. But Jacob learned gratuitousness from God, he learned to go beyond human categories: "I know, my son, I know." And he maintains his election.

Jacob had entered into God's mentality. Jacob was doing already what the "Magnificat" sings of: he overthrows the powerful—thrones, established situations, securities, sufficiencies, birth-rights, assurances of all kinds. God escapes human measures: he sends away the rich empty-handed, but fills the hungry with blessings . . . He exalts the lowly.

This reality, this divine "necessity," is so imperious that it will modify all history, leading to the rejection of the elected people—encrusted in Pharisaism—in favor of the Gentiles. The well-fed are left to their proud knowledge of the Law. And it is to the hungry that the good news is brought.

"The very stone which the builders rejected has become

the head of the corner. . . . Therefore I tell you, the kingdom of God will be taken away from you and given to a nation producing the fruits of it. When the chief priests and the Pharisees heard his parables, they perceived that he was speaking about them" (Mt. 21, 42–45).

And St. Paul says, "What shall we say, then? That Gentiles who did not pursue righteousness have attained it, that is, righteousness through faith; but that Israel who pursued the righteousness which is based on law did not succeed in fulfilling that law. Why? Because they did not pursue it through faith, but as if it were based on works. They have stumbled over the stumbling stone, as it is written . . ." (Rom. 9, 30).

This stumbling stone was the "scandal" of the gratuitous gift of God. This "faith" is the humble acceptance of being the beneficiary of this gift without having deserved it.

But let us be careful. If I say to myself, "I am the true younger son, beloved of God, I am not like these Pharisees who are doing good deeds, who go to daily Mass, who run around, who worry all the time about others, who try from morning till night to please the Lord. For myself, I do not go to Mass more than is required, I go to confession only once a year, I do not go running around to recollections, I do not think of the commandments . . . I am a publican, an authentic publican. God loves me!" —I become a Pharisee.

The Pharisaism of the satisfied publican is the worst of all, because it caricatures and parodies the new and eternal covenant. The ordinary Pharisaism merely disfigures the old covenant: conversion is still possible.

We must not believe in *any* way that our merits (even our merits the wrong way round!, that is to say, our faults) will assure us of eternal life. This is *the* sin of the Pharisees.

And there is still another discouraged Pharisaism which we practice more often perhaps than the triumphant Pharisaism which we have learned after all to guard against. This discouraged Pharisaism consists in believing that our demerits are the cause of all our troubles. To believe that we are condemned because we do not have any merit is to profess implicitly that we would be saved if we had some.

This familiar despair is but the reverse of Pharisaical self-sufficiency.

But then, you will say, What is to be believed, finally. What is to be thought?

We must say, Have pity on me, Lord, because I am a sinner . . . and we must "think" as little as possible. "Into your hands I commit my spirit."

We must say, Lord, I believe, come to the help of my unbelief. Lord, *you can* heal me. Lord, I know that I do not know anything. But I know also that you are Father, that you are able to create your Son in me. I know that I do not deserve anything—but that you will give me everything if only I trust you.

The scribes and the doctors of the Law could not stand it that this kind of prayer was preferred to their edifying recapitulations of meritorious works. The "sons of Abraham," the "do-gooders" of that time stumbled on this stumbling block.

And the first one to have been exasperated by this scandalous kindness of God is Cain. Cain is the first Pharisee—embittered to the point of killing this younger brother whose happy, humble, and filial innocence exasperated him.

*

In what way is Abel's sacrifice efficacious? What fecundity may such a death have?

The continuation of the story suggests it, and the New Testament will throw a full light on the value of "redemption" which is to be seen in it.

God has pity on Cain. He calls him, he makes a sign to him, Cain answers . . . what we answer all the time: "Am I my brother's keeper?" (One of the miracles of the Bible is that everything is told in it. All that we have done, all the evil we dream of doing, all our rage, all our ill-temper, all our blasphemies have been uttered. We will not do better. Everything has already been accomplished.)

"Cain said to the Lord, 'My punishment is greater than I

can bear' ": Cain succumbed to his jealousy. Notice, however,
that it is nowhere said that he was not loved. It is not said
that God *did not* love Cain. But on that particular day it
pleased God to consider Abel's offering with more joy; Abel
happened, on that morning, to make the heart of God happier.

And just as Adam could not stand a limit to his enjoyment
of the earthly paradise, so Cain could not stand a limit to the
favors he obtained from God.

Cain should have tolerated seeing his brother preferred.
But the narrow, petty, absurd love he felt led him to a crime.

Fortunately, Cain, once punished, does repent. And as soon
as he repents the sinner is forgiven, protected.

Protected with a sign, the Scriptures say. And this is the
beginning of a series of signs which will save: the sign of the
blood of the lamb saves the Hebrews in Egypt during the passover of the Lord. And we are, for our salvation, marked with
the sign of the cross, with the sign of the blood of our brother
crucified for us. It is given to us to be protected . . . with the
very sign of our greatest fault! St. Paul, in the Letter to the
Hebrews, speaks of "the sprinkled blood that speaks more
graciously than the blood of Abel" (12, 24).

Abel is an image of Christ. And Cain is the ancestor (ancestor and image at the same time) of the saved people, of
the protected people. "If anyone slays Cain, vengeance shall
be taken on him sevenfold" (Gen. 4, 15).

This point of the story marks a decisive turn in the history
of God's disposition towards men. It is the first dissociation
between merit and happiness, between obedience and life.
From Abel on, God shifts into reverse. Adam was punished
because he was bad. Here, it is the good man who is killed.
And the sinner, once forgiven, is marked with a sign which
protects him.

The story of Abel and Cain leads us to discover that God
does not reward good and punish evil on this earth; that
"God's justice" does not always happen right away and is not
always in line with our short-sighted views; that we have to

meditate this mystery: God leans with great pity over the sinner, but he lets the Innocent suffer.

*

What is this protective sign?

The Fathers of the Church, who always audaciously chose the interpretation according to the Spirit beyond time and space, taught that it was already a question of the sign of the cross.

The cross alone, in fact, can throw light on a destiny like Abel's. After the cross of Jesus, we can understand the meaning, the weight of such a death.

We know, since the ignominious execution of the most Just, that the Just must be treated as a sinner in order for the sinner to be treated as just! (Daniélou). We have been initiated into this mystery.

For it is a mystery. But how can one think it is a repulsive mystery? How can *we* think it is a repulsive mystery? Through which aberration are we sometimes tempted to prefer a regime where God's justice would be like ours, where the wicked would be struck down and everyone treated according to his own worth!

Do we not see that this is to wish our own destruction? Where is our chance of salvation? Is it not, precisely, in belonging to an order where the sinners are *forgiven?* —where a mysterious communion will raise, in spite of ourselves, our heaviness and our cowardice? Where all this evil we do is mysteriously redeemed, healed? Where we are saved *by* the suffering which those will have borne whom, precisely, our indifferences or our wickedness will have hurt so badly?

*

Only Jesus could endure everything. Only Jesus could bear everything without having committed anything and "without opening his mouth." Jesus' blood is the only perfectly innocent blood. That is why it speaks "more graciously than the blood of Abel."

Yet Abel's blood, from the dawn of sacred history, protests against all those who, throughout the centuries, want to identify unhappiness with punishment. "One only gets what one deserves." — "He had it coming." — "It was only to be expected."

A ferocious naïveté, which is far from having died out, insinuates to each of us—in joy but perhaps above all in sorrow—that it is indeed on this earth that God sooner or later rewards good and punishes evil. That if one is defeated, it is because one was wicked, that the unhappy are . . . guilty.

The best example of the kind is provided by Job's friends. Job: forsaken by his friends? Not at all. It would have been a lesser evil. On the contrary: Job surrounded by friends who bustle around him, who one after the other explain to him the cause of his troubles: "You must have done a whopper! To be in such a state, you really must have deceived yourself! The good man, the just . . . it is clear now! Your hypocrisy has finally come to an end. It was high time!", etc., etc. . . . One can easily imagine all the comments.

Now this usually takes place around a cup of coffee, and with a discreetly afflicted commiseration. But no one will ever be secure from this surprise: suddenly to see his friends come together in order to work him over, to sound his conscience, to lavish cutting bits of advice, barely beside the point, one more exasperating than the other, and this when he is at the end of his strength, when he is worn out, when he would need a little sympathy and love. This is Job's story.

And if we lack so cruelly charitable friends, there is somebody who is always ready to play this merciless role: ourselves. "What have I done wrong for this to be such a failure!" How many do not ask themselves this discouraging question after a defeat? It is the adult counterpart, the faithful echo, the resigned acceptation of the stupid "Little Jesus will punish you" which perhaps revolted us in our childhood, but which we have not been able to avoid adopting.

It is often in this way that false, stupid, revolting ideas triumph: through wear and tear. We reject them, storm, oppose them with words and shouts. But a fault in us servilely lets them penetrate, invade our own heart, our own judgment, modify our own outlook.

This condemnation—of our parents, of our friends—we refused it with our lips. But if our heart condemns us now, it is because we have not known how not to let ourselves be subdued by it. "The parents have eaten unripe grapes and their sons' teeth are set on edge."

In spite of all the adolescents' declarations of independence and emancipation, warped ideas, sad ideas, annihilating ideas . . . are handed down to them—intact. The form changes a little. But the original, profound prejudice remains ineradicable.

The "punishment of heaven" on the unhappy is one of the most execrable of these prejudices. It humiliates those who suffer. According to this point of view, one ends up with this detestable criterion: the unluckiest is probably the guiltiest (the laziest, the most improvident, the most financially irresponsible!). And the most prosperous? The most just? A good reputation, a promising career, a beautiful home . . . are certificates of virtue, —certificates of merit. And affliction, a change in fortune, is a "warning from heaven."

Those persons who "get what they deserve" are pleasure-seekers, materialists. They spend too much time on entertainment and not enough time in church. They "had it coming." They weren't "fulfilling their religious duties."

We are so used to giving back evil for evil that we annex God himself to this law of retaliation.

And this while we can see the contrary in sacred history, ever since the time of Abel, even in a certain way since the time of Adam. We see that sinners are *forgiven*. And that the "punished" are, generally, redeemers.

Surely he has borne our griefs
  and carried our sorrows;
Yet we esteemed him stricken,
  smitten by God, and afflicted.
But he was wounded for our transgressions, . . .
Upon him was the chastisement that made us whole,
  and with his stripes we are healed (Is. 53, 4-5).

Joseph, another figure of Christ: he feeds his brothers with the bread he has earned in exile, an exile caused by these very brothers' hardheartedness.

Job . . . is the only one to respect the mystery of his suffering, to believe that it is not a punishment, to hope for another explanation.

All of these sufferings of the just of the old covenant were to lead us to an understanding of and participation in the suffering of the most Just, the most Persecuted.

Since Christ, there is no longer need to grope like Job; the meaning of suffering is no longer a distressing problem, but merely a resemblance, a staggering election.

The innocent persecuted, the unhappy pure hearts, the afflicted, the misunderstood, the hounded . . . can recognize in Christ the holiest, the noblest image of what they have become.

The greatest love that God can express to us is to wish to see us share his condition, to wish us very close to him on the Calvary where those who are willing to follow him participate most closely in his task, in his work of redemption of the world.

To the good thief who accepted the fraternity of the crucifixion, who had a presentiment of its glory and of its joy, Jesus says, "*This very day*, you will be with me in paradise"—you will be with me in the resurrection, in the peace, in the love which, beyond distress and death, work to save the world.

Pius XI used to say: if you want to know what God thinks of earthly goods, see to whom he gives them. And see what he gives to those he loves most: the twelve apostles died martyrs or exiles. (And there is the savory episode of St. Teresa of Avila crossing a river and being nearly drowned. As she is grumbling a little against the Lord, he answers her, Teresa, don't you know that that is the way I treat my friends? And Teresa replies, Yes, Lord, and that is why you have so few of them!)

*

Another mystery is the reversibility of sufferings. It seems that it is possible to alleviate one suffering through another. "My life for yours" is no mere cliché. "I lay down my life *for* the sheep." — "Greater love has no man than this, that a man lay down his life *for* his friends" (Jn. 15, 13). Exchange? Bargain? Commerce? Obviously not. But it is difficult to determine exactly what takes place.* It is a mystery. A mystery of communion and participation—of union in one body.

* Let us try to clear several avenues:

(a) One does not suffer "instead of another," to exempt him from suffering and allow him to lead a careless and comfortable life! But to obtain for him the capability of suffering well, to increase his courage and his strength.

(b) One does not suffer "abstractly," as if a certain quantity of suffering were due (to whom?), and if I provide a greater quantity, another will owe less. This imagination caricatures God as a kind of Moloch, happy as long as he has his ration of suffering, whoever the provider may be.

(c) It is not a question of suffering, but of loving. Only love, being what is divine in the world, is, like God, universal, communicable, and efficacious.

This true love incites one to unite, to feel solidarity with the cause of those who suffer. But if one can understand the instinctive movement through which, incapable of remaining unharmed by the suffering of the others, we hasten to join them by the quickest, the shortest way, by imposing on ourselves a suffering which would be the token of the sincerity of our sympathy (for compassion does not long remain sincere in a body in full bloom), it is nonetheless to be desired that we not impose on ourselves useless sufferings (which hurt us without being useful to anybody), but that we seek to participate actively in the struggle against the suffering of the others. This sincere commitment will quickly make us share the condition from which we want to free them.

The nobleness of Christ's passion is that it was not a work of asceticism, a sought-after mortification, but merely the faithfulness of love.

To accept and to offer inevitable sufferings is to love God's will.

To impose on ourselves voluntary sufferings is to do our will and be reassured at small cost.

Your crosses must come from your apostolic commitments and not from your personal fabrication.

This suffering chosen as a testimony of love (instead of a love faithful even unto suffering) seems to me to be an invention of ascetics. Having fled from the world, from its temptations and its worries for a solitude or a "cloistered paradise," uneasy over the facil-

Any accepted suffering in this spirit *has* redemptive power. And even a power which can be directed, it seems. People have been helped, supported, perhaps saved, because, on a given day, somebody prayed and suffered "for them"—*with* them.

Somebody, in this anguish, has been close to them because he began, through love, to suffer like them.

Is there not some moral here which will get us out of our depression? "O foolish men!" Will we at last understand that suffering is an extraordinary power bestowed upon us, and not a mutilation? Not a failure, but a victory! —a victory over absence, separation, time and space, isolation, despair.

The body of Christ is we ourselves. The Messiah, henceforth, is we ourselves. Is it not necessary to go on "suffering all these things to enter into the glory," raising with us those whom the Father has committed to our care?

And in order to know "of what Spirit we are," let us learn, as did the disciples of Emmaus, "in all the Scriptures the things concerning himself" (and therefore concerning us as well).

---

ity of their life, they have racked their brains for these gratuitous mortifications which were a very poor replacement for those which their contemporaries would have generously provided them with, with the twofold advantage that they would not have had to choose them, and that they would have been useful to the others.

II

SACRIFICE AND MORTIFICATION

There are few words whose meaning is so misunderstood as that of the word *sacrifice*. Speak of sacrifice in a Christian assembly and all the faces cloud over, the temperature drops. Everybody begins to fear for what is dear to him: his pocketbook, his cigarettes, his entertainments, his parties. Everyone becomes afraid to think of God.

Now this word means first of all, not a deprivation, not a loss or a destruction, but a consecration: *sacrum facere*, to make sacred, to confer an infinite value.

Alas, one has only kept the painful and negative side of it, the side which concerns and interests us in all that is most selfish and smallest in us. For we are selfish even in our "sacrifices," and if it happens that we do not flee them, we manage at least to use them.

A "good Christian" who virtuously (and even without being in a bad mood) used to deprive himself of cigarettes during Lent, answered somebody who marvelled about it, "It keeps the will alive." For him as for many others, asceticism is a sport, a training through which a person improves his nerves, his will, his stomach, even his figure. And since it seems to please God, all the better. It is like killing two birds with one stone. You might as well "be ascetic" during this particular time of the year, or else it would seem that you lack perseverance. And having a double motive, you will have twice as much will power. God? Well, "he gives us the courage" to "be ascetic." We do it all as a "sacrifice."

Of course, asceticism should have a place in our life. But

it is always a moral activity. In itself, it is not religious. To deprive oneself of a permitted pleasure in order to be able to renounce a forbidden one, is a necessary discipline, an excellent hygiene, but one which is no more essentially religious than is fasting in order to lose weight.

Moreover, asceticism is not necessarily a pursuit of suffering either. On the contrary! The true modern asceticism seems to me to get enough sleep, to limit one's activities and hours of work to a reasonable measure ("If I were not so lazy, I wouldn't work so much!"), to nourish oneself calmly, and above all to relax healthily by taking part in leisurely pastimes which are not more exhausting than work!

We should not make God into some kind of means for our gaining inflexible will power. It is all too easy to make a torturer out of him. To many people, anything that is religious can only be disagreeable. A strange agreement on this point has been established between libertines and religious zealots. They admit the same principle, but make different applications of it. For all of them, religion is hostile to life, the supernatural is hostile to nature and God to joy. The zealots, in order to mortify themselves, live unpleasantly an unpleasant life which will guarantee them heaven. At least they believe so. For the libertines, since they prefer an agreeable life at once (A bird in the hand is worth two [God] in the bush), they resign themselves to be perfect pagans and philosophically renounce heaven. (Besides, the prospect of meeting there only the pious zealots makes the loss quite bearable.)

We terribly mistrust joy. As soon as a duty seems enjoyable, it appears questionable to us. Our true "duty" must be somewhere else. Our vocation does not seem worthy of this name if, by chance, it looks as if it were becoming gay. Vaguely anxious, we torture our heart and our mind until we have found a way sufficiently gloomy to be reassuring—sufficiently painful to be probably "pleasing to God."

But what do we take him for? What kind of idea do we have of God? (Many people would not like to be the God whom they imagine: they would be a better God.) Who thinks he pleases his mother by refusing the dish she offers?

Who thinks that he rejoices his father by throwing his gifts away? By what right do we think that God expects us to refuse his gifts, that he only offers us something because he knows that, in good conscience, we will have to turn it down? So many gifts from God, are they so many traps? What dark idea do we have of him?

We still obscurely believe in a gourmand, cannibal divinity —Nemesis, jealous of men—to whom one throws half of one's goods in order to save the other half. We resemble the ancient character who threw a golden ring into the sea to appease the gods. And then catching a fish, he finds his ring again. Horrors! He is lost. The gods do not want this small "sacrifice." Destiny is not avertible. Nothing could be more alarming than this good luck.

Our uneasiness before happiness is a survival of this old superstitious dread of man before a God assumed to be malicious and cruel. And these "sacrifices" which we throw him as fodder are the sign of a horrible mistrust—at the very time when he was precisely asking of us an increase in love, confidence, and joy.

The thing to destroy, "to mortify," is this fear, this obstinate tendency to protect ourselves from him, to defend ourselves by sacrifices of our choice against the invasion of his love.

This invasion is not an idea of ours, it thus frightens us. We do not know where it can lead, while abstinence on Friday during Lent . . . there at least we know what we commit ourselves to. There is nothing as reassuring as a rite. Nothing as delimited as a formalism. At least there, God has no chance of going beyond measure.

"I never eat meat on Friday in Lent." And you think that everything is all right. Didn't you ever read in your missal: "Is not this the fast that I choose . . . to share your bread with the hungry, and bring the homeless poor into your house; when you see the naked to cover him . . ." (Is. 58, 1–9. Reading of the first Friday of Lent).

"Do not believe," St. Augustine says, "that fast is sufficient in itself. Your deprivations will be fruitful for you if you make generous gifts to others." And St. Leo: "Let us take from what we ordinarily have something which will be of use to help the poor. And giving joy, you will yourself receive joy in return."

Your Lenten fish is as pagan as the hot-dog of your neighbor if it is not used to give a poor man the steak you deprive yourself of. If deprivation alone were agreeable to God, we would have been told: "Mortify one another. Make each other suffer" (which we do, but from our own initiative!), instead of "love one another."

God does not command us to save money, but to do acts of love and generosity.

Have we become so Pharisaical that we believe we please God by mortifications without love?

*

To sacrifice is to make sacred. Sacrifice is the act which valorizes the most on earth. But through a fearful selfishness, we have only retained the petty side of things, the side which allows one to say, when a man is sacrificed, sanctified, that he "lost" his profane character.

Any sacrament is a sacrifice. Take baptism. To baptize is to sacrifice, to consecrate a child. Baptism is a sacrifice, it makes somebody sacred. Through baptism a child passes from the sinful world into the communion of saints. Incorporated into Christ, he receives from him a new life, infinitely more precious than the life his parents transmitted to him. From then on he belongs to Christ, infinitely more than to them. He lives from the life of Christ more than from their life. This is indeed a sacrifice, but is there greater joy?

Marriage is a sacrifice. Be careful, —not a sacrifice in the sense in which you think of it. But all married people know well that something essential to their love would be lacking if their engagements were purely profane, if they did not make of them a sacred thing, a sacrament. And as at the marriage of Cana Christ changed the water, which the spouses in their poverty were ashamed of, into wine, so they ask him to change their human and profane love into his tireless love.

At the marriage, the husband sacrifices his wife and the wife her husband. From then on, Christ makes a third in their love: "That they be one, in us," in order to give them the capability of loving each other as he loves them, and as they are by themselves incapable of loving each other.

Marriage is intended to make a natural love pass (Easter is a passover) into the supernatural order. Each one has sacrificed in it his selfishness, his cowardice, his weakness, but who would dare to say that he has lost something in it?

When a young girl enters a convent, everyone takes pity or goes into ecstasies over her "renunciations." What a scandal, to consider above all in a gift the renunciations which it entails. Have you ever heard of a married couple enumerating to one another the "opportunities," the advantages, the people they have "sacrificed" by marrying one another?

Between God and man, between God's love and man's selfishness, between the world of light and the world of the prince of darkness, there is only one bridge, one communication, one passage, one possible passover: sacrifice.

Sacrifice is the great work of joy, the filial act par excellence, the act through which a profane thing becomes sacred, a lost being can find himself again, a temporal thing becomes eternal, something soiled is consecrated.

God's joy is to give himself, the joy of the creature is to give himself up.

God has created everything in love, that is to say, in unity.

The devil is he who divides: man from God, wife from husband, nature from its master, man from his own body (he was ashamed of it, he did not recognize himself any more in it, he was afraid to find it so different from himself), sons from one another (Abel and Cain), children from parents (Noah and his sons). And the peoples are scattered all over the earth (Babel), separated from one another by barriers or iron curtains, color, race, class, or culture curtains, while the wish of God is: "That they be one even as we are one."

Sin is atoned for only through sacrifice. What was in the beginning gift and *élan* has become restitution. But the joy of the return is incomparably greater than the regret for what one leaves behind. And the reparation is so perfect that it restores the integrity, the original innocence. Sacrifice is above all an act of joy: "I do as the Father has commanded me, so that the world may know that I love the Father" (Jn. 14, 31). "But now I am coming to thee; and these things I speak in the world, that they may have my joy fulfilled in themselves" (Jn. 17, 13).

"When he was crucified, Christ merely accomplished on this earth, in his distant provinces, amidst the tumult of the elements, what he does unceasingly in his house, in glory and in joy." He gave thanks, he committed himself into the hands of his Father. One time, in the succession of centuries, heaven opened and we contemplated the eternal beatitude of God, the intensity of his joy, the strength with which he knows how to love, and we have called it crucifixion, passion, cross, sacrifice.

*

It is because a true sacrifice is an act of love and joy that our Lord instituted the Eucharist during a meal. The relation between the Last Supper and Calvary (between the idea "meal" and the idea "sacrifice"), is naturally difficult to grasp for all those who identify sacrifice with deprivation: for how can a fraternal meal be reconciled with a sacrifice? This is, however, the mystery of the Mass, and, besides, the central rite of any religion.

A meal is a time when people learn to love each other. It is around a table that friends perceive best, without having to explain it, the warmth of being together. It is at table that fraternity expresses, creates or strengthens itself.

Children learn, at meals, to know their parents' love. These happy, these good family meals which the mother spends her life, *gives her life* to prepare, to make a success of, which the father spends his life, *gives his life* to afford, are the place of communion of the children in the love of their parents. The family intimacy, the family spirit is created there, nourishes itself there so well that, later on, when the family is dispersed, it will be the only thing which will bring the family together: they will celebrate a meal together.

The meal sanctifies the children through the sacrifice of the parents; the love of the latter arouses the love of the former (see Jn. 17, 19). The children learn to love with the very love with which they are loved.

And it is at table that the disciples of Emmaus recognized the Lord: "at the breaking of the bread," at this gesture of love, through which, instead of helping himself, he broke his bread and gave it to them.

At the Last Supper our Lord revealed his bread, revealed the gift of his life. It was the *same* act as on Calvary. "Greater love has no man than this, that a man lay down his life . . ." He who gives his bread, gives his life. It was the same Gift, the same Joy. "I have earnestly desired to eat this passover with you before I suffer" (Lk. 22, 15).

The most joyful act on earth includes a secondary painful side (work of the mother, possible deprivation, etc.), but this disappears so much before the radiance of joy *if* one loves.

The meal around which all the children will soon warm themselves, meet together again, brighten up, costs the mother pain, work, worry, but she does not even think of it, so little is it beside the happiness of seeing them happy together.

To count one's sacrifices, to make them into "spiritual bouquets," is to turn God into a kind of Moloch, and to use him as a means, —as the boring means of our moral perfection. We will never become religious by offering spiritual bouquets. We will never meet God if we have to count our way.

Any true love engenders sacrifice, but any sacrifice does not engender love. God is not sacrifice. God is love. And because he is love, he has become sacrifice—joyful sacrifice.

When one serves the children at table, or one's friends at a fraternal meeting . . . one forgets to eat. So pleasant is it to care for them, so much more pleasant than to eat. Who will have the feeling of having "made a sacrifice"?

When one loves, one is (necessarily) led to fast—without even thinking of it. But when one fasts in order to suffer . . .

it is difficult to imagine that it leads us to love—or to be happy.

To forego eating a steak is sad, but to serve a steak—what a joy!

It is always the same thing. "If any one says, 'I love God,' and hates his brother, he is a liar; for he who does not love his brother whom he has seen, cannot love God whom he has not seen" (1 Jn. 4, 20). He who pretends to fast "for" God whom he has not seen and who does not know how to fast for a brother whom he has seen . . .

Christ's fast in the desert? It was in order to pray. It was because he preferred to talk with his Father. And the Gospel tells us that he became hungry only when he had finished praying. Who among us does not prefer the conversation of a loved one to the eating of a fine meal?

To attribute to suffering a value in itself is fakirism—or sport—or stoicism.

Christ was not at all a stoic. He said he was thirsty. He complained about being left alone. He let himself be helped under his cross. He did not feel any joy in mastering himself. About the fast that his disciples do not observe, he says, "Can you make wedding guests fast while the bridegroom is with them?" (Lk. 5, 34).

We will not find any systematic asceticism in Jesus. Nor any formalism. "Not what goes into the mouth defiles a man . . ." (Mt. 15, 10). "Go and learn what this means, 'I desire mercy and not sacrifice'" (Mt. 9, 13).

He knew very well that mercy leads to sacrifice. He knew very well to what sacrifice his mercy would lead.

*

Christian education is above all education in the paternity of God, and not in sacrifice; in God's love for us, and not in our love for God; in what God does for us, and not in what we do for God.

God loves us. God loves us when we do not love him yet, and when we love him no longer. God loves us as sinners. Would he love men if he did not love them as sinners? God does not need our merits or our sacrifices in order to love us.

God does not love us because of our virtues. He loves us in spite of us. God is the Father. To be the Father is to take the initiative in loving. The Christian religion consists in the first place, St. John tells us, not so much in the fact that we love God, but that God has loved us first.

Nothing is more dangerous than premature mortification, sacrifices, all that would lead us to try to merit God's love, to compete with God's generosity before we have understood it. There is nothing more Pharisaical than to want to make ourselves worthy of God's love before we have admitted that he loves us unworthy.

If this truth is obscured, God very quickly becomes the one who receives, instead of the one who gives, the one who takes, instead of the one who gives the capacity of giving. And then, man takes the place of God, he becomes better than the God he imagines. When he thinks of God, either he is afraid of the sacrifices God is going to ask from him, and he avoids as much as possible fixing his thought on him; or he remembers his own sacrifices rather than God's blessings, and he gradually begins to think of himself as a kind of hard pressed benefactor of God. Some of us, when we recall our past, say to ourselves, "All that I have done for God! All that I have sacrificed for him! But what has he done for me?" It is fortunate when we do not regret it!

The child, willingly a bookkeeper, a jurist, naïvely interested, practical, Judaizing, will readily fill his "sacrifice notebooks" and will accumulate his merits without gaining in true generosity, nor above all in love of God.

God created the world with everything which is beautiful and good in it. He rejoices when we appreciate his gifts. It is to pay homage to him if one finds his work good. He has done everything so that we may enjoy and find, in his creation, a testimony and a reflection of his goodness. He entrusts it to us without regret, without bitterness. And when somebody has found it good, God rejoices at having met, finally, a man of the same opinion as himself: "And God saw that it was good."

God does not need our sacrifices. He does not like his children to torment themselves, hurt themselves, become gloomy. He loves only to give, and if he calls us to loving and voluntary sacrifice, it is because he is so much a Father that he wants us to share everything: he wants to invite us to know his joy, to imitate his generosity. He wants to give us the capacity of giving.

By dint of giving, he teaches us to give. The Father would not be completely Father if he did not give us the capacity of giving. For if he gave us only the capacity of receiving, he would give us nothing of himself: he is not "receiving." He is giving and love. Then, when he wants totally to entrust us with his being and his tastes, he gives us the capacity of becoming Father in our turn, he gives us the capacity of giving.

It is from God that we have to learn how to give. First it is necessary to immerge oneself in, to steep oneself in, to let oneself be penetrated by the infinite goodness, the amazing generosity of God. We will never be persuaded enough of it. We will never be through with learning how kind, how tender, how exceedingly generous God is.

The filial prayer par excellence is: "Father, I know that you always hear me." Who among us would dare to say that? But who believes he is really a son, and would dare not to say it? To believe in the Father, is exactly to believe that he always hears our prayer, and even far beyond the request.

The filial attitude can be defined through these words: "Father, everything which is yours is mine." Everything begins with that, with the initiation into the infinite paternal generosity. Even to the bitter elder son, the father of the prodigal son speaks in this way: "Son, you are always with me, and all that is mine is yours."

And it is when you believe this, when you are invaded and penetrated by the Father's love, that you can add, "And everything that is mine is yours."

Then this affirmation is not a presumption and a boast, it is but total fidelity. If one has received what is the Father's, one has received the capacity to do as he does: to give.

The worst blasphemy is to inverse the terms and to begin religion with our sacrifices. One says to God, "What is mine is yours." And then one adds, "So please give me something of yours." One usurps the place of God. One takes the initiative of love. One becomes the father of God. And then one advises him to be as kind as we are, to make an effort in order to raise himself to the height of our sacrifices. Everything is false in this attitude: we set ourselves up as benefactors of God. We raise ourselves onto a pedestal. And God seems inert, indifferent, passive, under obligation.

One of my students, every Lent, used to try to offer to God the sacrifice of not smoking. He would get into a very bad mood, become irritated, begin sucking on candy and eating chocolates, "since he had promised not to smoke, but did not promise not to eat candy," eventually let himself be tempted by friends to resume smoking, and finished Lent demoralized, angry against God and against himself.

At the beginning of one Lenten season he came to see me and asked, "What should I do for mortification?" — "I don't know," I said. "What do you suggest?"

He looked at me with a shy air. "I could maybe try not to smoke?" — "Ah no, you have been boring us for years with that. You will rather do the contrary. You will smoke, but you will make a sacrifice of each of your cigarettes. You will smoke them to the glory of God, thanking him for having created things as good as tobacco." —He thought first that I was making fun of him. A solid Christian education persuaded him that nothing agreeable could really be religious. I had to expend floods of eloquence before he could be convinced that he could please God by smoking, and that the smoke of his cigarettes would be as spirals of incense of agreeable odor. Three weeks later he came back. "Well, what news?" — "It's going very well, I don't smoke any more." — "You're impossible. When you were not supposed to smoke you did. Now that you chose to smoke, you don't smoke any more." — "Well, Father," he said, "I will explain. First, I have to confess that I had a great deal of trouble smoking for the glory of God, pretend or feel that something was religious which seemed to me so worldly. And even when I succeeded, imagine that these first cigarettes didn't please me. I discovered

then that when I used to smoke, until then, it was an absolutely pagan act, a kind of revenge which I took against all
that is imposed and obligatory. I would send everything to
the devil and give myself a pleasure, taking a slice of good
time in a boring life. The real pleasure of smoking was to
send duty on vacation, to taste a solitude, a freedom whose
final end must be vaguely the pleasure of damnation (withdrawal, excommunication, absolute emancipation).

"And then, little by little, I got used to it and I really
smoked a few cigarettes with filial feeling. First, I had to
struggle against the impression that God was not pleased with
me. I had a bad conscience from enjoying this pleasure during
Lent. I used to think of God only for mortifying myself. But
after a while, I came to think that God offered me a cigarette,
that I pleased him in accepting it, that I smoked it to his
glory, and that this pleasure, far from separating me from
him, introduced me into his intimacy.

"Then, at a certain moment, the thought that I could
smoke, that God was glad that I smoked, that he invited me
paternally to do so, rejoiced me so much, put me in such a
state of gladness and peace, that I no longer needed to smoke.
I went on thinking of God and was happier that way. Our
relations were purer. The cigarette would have distracted
me."*

Let us not start, therefore, with sacrifice, mortification, the
cross. It is only when you are quite persuaded that God loves
you, for nothing, always, in any case, without merit, before
any sacrifice, that this love once learned and slowly infused
will be able to accomplish its works in you. "The Father, who
is in me, does himself his works."

Look at the Gospel. It begins with an immense gladness:
promises, announcements, miracles, calls, friendships, wonders, the presence and the tenderness of God for us. What

* We must carefully distinguish between moral asceticism (with its
dangers of withdrawal and self-affirmation), and spiritual asceticism
(a certain sensitivity to that which, in us, harms or favors divine life,
and which is an exercise in thoughtfulness and self-effacement. "Do
not grieve the Holy Spirit," St. Paul says.).

we had first to learn, the most urgent message, is that God is infinitely kinder, infinitely tenderer, gayer, younger, more favorable than what we had ever imagined. The great, the most urgent duty was to exult, to give thanks, to wonder, to be overwhelmed and then exalted, to cry and to laugh, to kiss his hands and his feet, to stop in order to know it, and then to begin over again. Ah! all our sacrifices were worth nothing, then, made as they were in pain, in lethargy, in the mistaken belief that we were alone, and sometimes finding ourselves better than the God for whom they were made? We used to do this good too badly, we were not worthy of the good we were doing. This good used to do us harm.

Jesus came to spread joy. All of those persons who opened themselves to him, who let themselves be won to his love, he filled them with his joy, he wanted them to abound with joy.

Christ does not speak, at the beginning, of sacrifice, of the passion, of the cross. It is necessary first to learn well, it is necessary first to know well who he is, to be penetrated by his goodness, by his love, by the joy of his tenderness; and then, but only then, everything follows. Slowly, love becomes aware of itself, of its strength, of its exigency. It feels itself growing, ripening for virile tasks, for more audacious loves. It knows better what it is and whom it loves. It desires more purely to say it. It restricts itself to the essential. It wants less to sing and more to act. It becomes consuming, ambitious, insatiable, so much is it supported with joy. It then conceives, it begins to understand what would be the testimony sufficient to such a joy. Finally, it lets itself be invaded by the appeasement of not being able to go beyond this love, of having been worthy of knowing and of exercising the greatest love. And it puts its Joy on the cross!

Love goes up with its joy onto the cross, in order to declare it, to affirm it, so that nobody could doubt it, to be finally relieved to have expressed it so well, to have expressed it so thoroughly with its blood, its tears, its cries, its prayers, and its immeasurable peace.

Jesus went up with his joy onto the cross: "I do as the Father has commanded me, so that the world may know that

I love the Father." He has shown what a son can do through enthusiasm for his father.

He crucified only his joy.

It is not God who needs our sacrifices, but we need to show him that we love him, and this strengthens our love.

Sacrifice is indispensable to love in order to express it and to purify it. But love is much more necessary yet to sacrifice. It is a question of a spiral, but its starting point is an initiative of God. It is only after having wondered at and been penetrated with God's prodigious kindness towards us, that we are able to let ourselves be won by it to the point of beginning to imitate it.

The religion which begins with sacrifice and the religion which does not end in it are equally to be condemned. What many lack in order to love God is certainly first of all to know his love and what he has done for us. But it is also, often, to have known how to respond to him by doing something for him. Devotion is a source of love after having been its fruit. Ask a mother why she really loves her child so much: it is because she has done so much for him. Very often, adolescents easily envisage death and seem not to hold onto life. It is seldom through virtue and love of heaven, but rather because they have done almost nothing yet for life and are not attached to it. In our religious life, the reason for our remaining so cold, so sluggish towards God, is not that he fails to coddle us, to smile on us, but it is that this kindness does not awaken any echo in our too hardened hearts. We have trouble believing in God's generosity because we are too selfish. One only really understands those whom one resembles. God does not cease giving, but since we never give him anything, we do not have in us the feeling which would unite us with him, by making us experience what it is to give, to love, to commiserate.

Badly educated children are not those for whom one has done too much. One never does too much for a child. But they are those who have never been taught to give back in exchange for what they have received. Parents who have spoiled their children are selfish people. They really did not give themselves. They kept for themselves what was best in them. They did not confide in them the joy of giving.

Sacrifice is necessary, but one must only sacrifice through love. Sacrifice is not what costs us a painful and rancorous renouncement, a destruction, an immolation, a dead loss (sacrificed soldiers! sacrificed goods! "The firm does not hesitate to make any sacrifice." — "I make little sacrifices.").

It is just the contrary. The most joyful and happiest act in the world is to enter into the divine world of generosity and love, to enter into God's game which is to give, to become capable of love and giving.

Poverty is not to become one's own executioner by snatching one's goods out of one's hands, it is to have found a better wealth which dispenses you from being rich.

Anything which is not offered is lost. How, therefore, is a particular moment in our day to be eternalized? Is it going to pass, to disappear for ever? No, there is a means of holding on to it, we can make of it something durable, integrated into our eternity, a source of happiness for ever. It suffices to sacrifice it, to make of it an act of charity. We will live eternally only those moments lived with love during our earthly life. What we usually mean by "merit" seems to me to be the means of eternalizing moments, things, and beings we would like to enjoy for ever.

To sacrifice is to be so much attached to God as to entrust him with what is dearest to us, in order for everything we love to be under the same care and on the same side.

There is a means of giving back to God everything he has given us, through expressing to him the confidence we have in him that he will keep it infinitely better than we would be able to. What we keep falls apart in our hands which retain it. But anything which is given to God is saved for ever.

Can we do less for somebody we love than to sacrifice him, to divinize him in this way?

III

THE SACREDNESS OF SUFFERING

The parable of the good seed and the weeds (Mt. 13, 24–30) shows the role God confers upon suffering and even upon sin. "Do not gather the weeds lest in gathering them you root up the wheat along with them."

But how will it play this role?

It is important to see suffering aright, to receive it and to bear it aright. Now men have found different ways of facing it which deprive it completely of the divine efficacy of which it was capable, with which it was laden.

A first way of "bungling" our suffering is to be a stoic.

What does the stoic do? He tries to master suffering. He practices an habitual and hardening asceticism which permits him to be "master of himself" in any circumstances. He anesthetizes himself. He desensitizes himself.

All of us have dreamt of being one of those tragical heroes, noble and imperturbable: "Suffering, you are but a word!"

One dreams of becoming insensitive to one's pain, and therefore, inevitably, one also becomes insensitive to the pain of others.

A certain asceticism is good, of course. Some troubles must only be treated with contempt. "Train yourselves for voluntary sufferings in order to be capable, one day, of accepting necessary sufferings without shipwreck." That is wise. That is sane. That is a salutary preventive moral hygiene. But it is not "religious" as such.

We should not believe that we rejoice God's heart *because*

we walk for x number of hours every week with stones in our socks.

If we do walk x number of hours every week for the love of our neighbor, in spite of the inevitable stones in our socks, we rejoice God's heart! And if, foreseeing *this* necessity, we train a little the soles of our feet *while thinking* not of our spiritual progress, but *of the neighbor* who will be able to benefit from this training . . . we rejoice God's heart.

For the concrete love which inspires them can alone make such gestures agreeable to God.

But love is a gift of God, and the more hard-shelled are the slowest to be penetrated by this grace. Education should thus never tend to harden children. One should not make them impermeable, one should not try to protect them from suffering.

They should, on the contrary, be taught to open themselves to it. If they are sensitive they will be exposed to much suffering, but they will be able to recognize in it the divine message, the marvelous increase in revelation which God reserves to his beloved.

*

Besides the stoics, there are the rebels.

Modern man thinks he has discovered in revolt the only dynamism which can allow him to fulfill himself. For him, evil and suffering prove that God does not exist and are, therefore, the occasion of his liberation.

But this revolt coincides curiously with an acute sense of the solidarity of all men. It is the most beautiful message which the work of Camus, for example, brings us. Men worthy of the name do not want to escape suffering in order not to "drop" the majority of their human brothers—who suffer.

The solidarity of Abel and Cain is perceived by our contemporaries. Nobody—Christian or atheist—would any longer dare to say, "I am not my brother's keeper." Underdeveloped countries, underdeveloped social classes, the handicapped of all kinds: there is none of these miseries which we have not learned to feel a solidarity with, which we have not learned to feel even a responsibility for.

An increased sense of human solidarity can be explained by more communication among men, by a broadening to a planetary scale of news coverage, of relations and exchanges of all kinds, by the cosmic way of envisaging existence.

Technical progress has engendered the atomic threat . . . but also this possibility of universal commiseration.

Péguy—but he had not many followers—wrote as early as 1902, "A single misery suffices to condemn a society. It suffices that a single man be kept or knowingly left in need for the entire civil contract to be null and void. As long as there is one man outside, the door which is closed in his face encloses a city of injustice and hatred."

Our time is very romantic. It sees as "black" as our grandfathers saw "rose-colored" fifty years ago. "Each time a school is opened, a prison can be closed," the naïve optimists in 1900 used to say. There are no worse pessimists than disappointed optimists.

The grandchildren of these announcers of "good days to come" are men in revolt, rebellion; and their despair is as naïve, as exaggerated, as yesteryear's delight.

There is something in this rebellion against the times that is artificial, even when its cause or object is perfectly genuine. (Civil rights, for instance; and I am thinking of the beautiful passage in Camus' *The Plague* when Rieux, the doctor, powerless, witnesses the long death-agony of a child.)

Today's men in revolt, as it were overwhelmed by the instinctive pain of the sight of suffering, are unable to examine the problem of the co-existence of good and evil . . . which would call everything into question again. One reasons, reacts as if everything were bad. It is not so simple. A single truly beautiful thing, a single truly good person, is sufficient to prove God. The existence of evil poses a problem, but it is powerless against the evidence of good, which it cannot explain. Out of pure evil one cannot draw good. But out of good, because of freedom, evil can arise.

Such an attitude, generous but blind and unreasonable, is

like that of adolescents, disappointed by their parents, who from then on condemn them totally and do not want to remember anything but the evil which, suddenly, they perceived too painfully. Even if they die of the sorrow of this disappointment. And this death itself would please them, for it would make the scandal of this frustration more obvious.

*

Revolt in face of the suffering of the world is an incomplete, impulsive reaction, too sentimental and not mature enough. It is, however, infinitely sounder than resignation.

The resigned—who are generally those well provided for—find an irritating justification in the intellectual security of certain philosophical systems for which suffering is one indispensable cog.

If one listens to them, everything is for the best in the best possible world. There is not a grinding which cannot be explained. The capacity for suffering is the necessary reverse of the capacity for joy.

And then—another astuteness—does not the unhappiness of one make for the happiness of another? For cyclists: the uphill for one will be the downhill for the other. The beam which will fall on your head is so heavy only because its blessed solidity has been supporting your grandmother's ceiling for a hundred years, etc. As for moral suffering, it is, they say, the source of all progress.

Without the good spring of moral suffering, the world would stagnate. The ideal creation which in our unconsciousness we have sometimes dreamt of perhaps, would lead, they tell us, to . . . stultification, moral death. Being established in security and happiness would lead us after a short time to a horrible laxness and unconcern. It would make of us a mass of satisfied, inert moral imbeciles.

If one does not begin by recalling and admitting the mystery of original sin, this philosophy is exasperating. The alarm signal . . . could really be more discreet! One could very well imagine beams at once solid and light, and a sufficient diffusion of light motor-cycles would make it possible that the exhaustion from pedaling uphill would not be the necessary ransom for the delight of coasting downhill! As for the spring of moral suffering, we would joyfully accept the idea of being propelled in a gentler way.

Besides, there will always be evidently useless (philosophically speaking), inexplicable, and even harmful and odious sufferings: oppression of the weak by the strong, the suffering of children . . .

*

Philosophy explains also—and better—the origin of sin.

The explanation of sin is in the liberty of man. It is easy to admit that freedom is the condition for love and that freedom implies a risk.

If one wants to be related to God through an adhesion of love, this presupposes a free choice. One can choose to love, to commit oneself to somebody only if one had the possibility of refusing, of withdrawing.

It is easy to imagine the sadness of a world where man would serve God with the punctuality of a robot—and to prefer our world, as it is.

But could not God guarantee the harmonious exercise of this liberty, ensure man a system of fast warning signals in order to keep him from wandering in dangerous paths?

The preservative blessings of a providence which would guarantee immediate penalties would be paid for by a dreadful impoverishment: we would have an impeccable but terrorized and sterile world—a world of slaves who would serve God only through fear or interest.

And it is not in this way that God imagined the salvation of the world. God did not suppress risk. He came to take the risk with us. God did not suppress sin. He invented forgiving it.

God is not afraid of sin. He has been at work in it since the beginning of the world! His masterpiece is to have made a beatitude of it: *"felix culpa"*! Let us understand: it is a beginning of beatitude, an introduction to beatitude, the only means, sometimes, of opening us to *his* beatitude.

The first effect of the presence of the Holy Spirit in a person is that he recognizes himself as a sinner (Jn. 16, 8).

A Jesuit friend of mine who had been sent to a Nazi extermination camp once told me that during a forced march, one of his companions and he had joined together in order to struggle against exhaustion. They went arm-in-arm. And he felt the arm of the other slide more and more under his, until the moment when, in the half-torpor into which tiredness had plunged him, he suddenly noticed that there was no longer any arm under his. His companion had fallen like so many others. And he, after a second of hesitation, went on without looking back.

Here is the type of an excessive suffering, so excessive that it seems to brutalize, to annihilate, to degrade.

It was this suffering, however, that taught this man how poor he was, how worthless, how powerless, how contemptible he could become without the help to which he *had* to appeal.

This memory, which will henceforth accompany him everywhere, has given him forever the "soul of a poor man." To measure one's own complete incapacity is a grace which some of us reach only through such an experience of distress and shame.

*

El Hallaj, an Arabian mystic and, mysteriously, a figure of Christ, crucified like his unknown master for having preached a doctrine of love, wrote:

"When God loves a servant, he incites others to persecute him in order for this servant to come and draw close to him alone."

*

The Old Testament tells us already that pain is a trial and not a punishment: "The Lord reproves *him whom he loves*, as a father the son in whom he delights" (Prv. 3, 12). Let us also recall Job's story. And Tobit: "Because you were agreeable to God, you had to be tried through suffering" (Tob. 12, 13).

The New Testament proclaims it to us at each page. A

good work to do in a community would be to search out all the passages which speak of suffering.

What does Jesus say about it?

In John 5, 14, to the invalid whom he just healed, he says, "Sin no more, that nothing worse befall you."

Christ seems indeed to affirm here that there is a link between sin and misfortune.

But let us be careful! If there is a link *there is not a proportion*. We find this in Luke 13, 1 ff. In this dialogue, Jesus begins by protesting: "Do you think that these Galileans were worse sinners than all the other Galileans, because they suffered thus? I tell you, no." Jesus is there answering patiently to the relating of news items by his entourage, accepting their poor level of conversation to draw from it, nevertheless, a lesson, to bring them, starting from their petty preoccupations, a little closer to his world.

These unfortunate Galileans are not then more guilty than the others. However Jesus adds: "Unless you repent, you will all likewise perish." If there is individually no direct and proportionate relation between sin and misfortune, we must nevertheless see in the latter a call to personal penance (that is to say, to personal conversion). And this in a perspective of solidarity ("Unless . . . you will *all* perish").

The story of the man born blind (Jn. 9) raises, from the first verse, the same problem.

The apostles, curious and cruel, with the concierge mentality which we all have, ask Jesus when they see this unfortunate man on the side of the road: "Rabbi, who sinned, this man or his parents, that he was born blind?"

Jesus answers, "It was not that this man sinned, or his parents, but that the works of God might be made manifest in him." Here is the great answer. Such is the richest and the most beautiful meaning of all our adversities.

"This illness is not unto death," Jesus says, "it is for the glory of God" (Jn. 11, 4).

Our sufferings are the support, the material of a "sign" of God. They all are "significant"—but it is sometimes necessary for us to wait, in lasting patience, for the significance of it to be given *to us*. And this, a long while. How old was the man born blind? How many years of absurd blindness, of incomprehensible darkness, that the joy of the pool of Siloam might burst out?

We must, in faith, see promises in our sufferings, and not mutilations. God weaves a masterpiece which we will discover only on the last day.

The parable of the vine and the branches also reminds us that if the sterile branches are cut and thrown away, "every branch that does bear fruit (the Father) prunes that it may bear more fruit" (Jn. 15, 2). And one must have worked in a vineyard to know how little is left after pruning!

When we feel the cut, the painful cracking from the pruning-shears . . . is it for our suppression or for our pruning? Who can distinguish? At the very moment, it hurts the same way.

But if our heart "abides in him," he promised us that he would abide in us and that we would bear "much fruit."

"My beloved speaks and says to me: 'Arise, my love, my fair one, and come away; for lo, the winter is past, the rain is over and gone. The flowers appear on the earth . . . the voice of the turtledove is heard on our land . . . the vines are in blossom'" (Song 2, 10).

We must accept the mystery of this pruning and believe in the joy of the harvest.

Is not the life of Jesus itself all pruning and painful growing?

Jesus is a conscious, total, voluntary Abel. He is the sorrowful lamb which bears the sins of the world, he is the suffering servant.

Jesus did not come to suppress suffering all at once, nor to explain it, nor to justify it. He came to assume it and to transform it. Bearing it with infinite love, he taught us how to relieve others of theirs and to patiently endure that which remains unavoidable, with him and in him.

Faithful, confident, committed to the Father even in death, he taught us that it is possible to be happy in unhappiness. Jesus, speaking of the fullness of his joy just before his passion, revealed to us that the latter did not exclude the former. "I do as the Father has commanded me, so that the world may know that I love the Father" (Jn. 14, 31). The way of the cross, for Jesus, was also a way of joy, of enthusiasm.

From the depth of his filial joy, he assumed human suffering in order to unite them forever. The espousal of St. Francis with Lady Poverty is but a secular translation of the espousal of Christ with suffering.

To welcome Christ's love is thus to espouse his suffering— *and* his joy: "blessed passion."

We should not end up by saying, however, that suffering comes from God. God does not punish men. Men punish themselves. God does not send misfortune and chastisements. The wickedness of men suffices to explain evil. Far from wanting to avenge himself on us, God weeps over our crimes and their consequences on us and on our descendants (Lk. 19, 44-45).

Even at the origin of the world, God made man capable of happiness through his intelligent work and his love. At each stage of his creation, God proclaims that what he is doing is good.

But man missed his entry into this Joy, and God, instead of punishing this failure, wanted to share and progressively redress the consequences.

Let us then not look for a divine *origin* of suffering: "What have I done to God that he sends me this trial?", but for a divine *use*: "How can I make of it an act of faith and love?"

God asks from us an infinite respect towards those who are suffering. Before all suffering, let us adore the mystery of God who proposes himself to man.

God asks us to believe that any suffering may become that of Christ—that it is *his* passion which continues ("In my flesh I complete what is lacking in Christ's afflictions," says St. Paul). What wounds him, what makes his work miscarry in us, is if we despair, if we let ourselves be humiliated, engulfed by suffering, if we despise this conformity with him which is the most beautiful thing he has to offer us.

There is no "unworthy" suffering, there is no cross which

does not resemble his. The good thief had committed more shameful faults than ours and he dared to speak to him, he dared to take advantage of the closeness of their torture. And Christ loved him, and they entered together into paradise.

Upon our crosses whatever they be, we should feel this loving look of the Lord, this look as anxious, as sorrowfully attentive, as impatient, as distressed, as compassionate as the look of the Father upon his crucified Son.

Suffering is sacred because it confers upon those whom it rends the most intimate resemblance to the sorrowful Son whose cross saves the world. The greatest quartering is the most faithful configuration to the Lord. A tortured heart committed to the Father, is the most living image of the Redeemer.

This suffering, this passion, makes of us beloved sons with whom the Father is well pleased. If we do not suffer, it means that we are not yet sons with the Son, saviours with the Saviour. It means that we are not ready, not alive enough. It means that the work of life has slowed down in us and that we are no longer capable of being pruned.

We must pray: Father, thy will be done; Father, that the vine be pruned as it should be in order to bear the fruit you expect from it; Father, thy will be done and not mine.

And when Jesus had prayed this way, the Gospel says, an angel appeared and comforted him (Lk. 22, 43).

✧ IV ✧

REDEMPTION
THROUGH SUFFERING

What is the sense of suffering? What sense is to be given to all this evil? What is the sense of the beatitude of the unfortunate? "Blessed are those who mourn . . ."

"Those who mourn" are those who, like Abel implicitly or Jesus in full consciousness, give life to their brothers through their suffering.

The reading of the Mass of the Good Shepherd begins with these words: "Beloved, Christ also suffered for you, leaving you an example, that you should follow in his steps" (1 Pet. 2, 21).

George MacDonald has said, "The Son of God suffered unto death, not that men might not suffer, but that their suffering might be like His."

And St. Peter affirms again: "By his wounds you have been healed." These words are very simple. But the thought they suggest is difficult. Why did Christ have to suffer this way? Why is redemption efficacious only through suffering?

Must we then believe in a vengeful God? In a cruel God? Is it really a question of "appeasing his anger"? So many quarts of blood per quantity of original sin? And if he does not find it in the offender, he seeks it at least in the innocent!

The meaning of the redemption is, unconsciously, reduced to this dull canvas in too many Christian consciences.

Too many Christians still believe that suffering has a value in itself. But then, why did not Christ say: "Make one another suffer" rather than "Love one another?" Notice that he did not even content himself with saying: "Serve one an-

other," or "Devote yourselves to one another," or "Do as if
you loved one another." He commanded. He dared to demand: *Love* one another.

All the theologians agree in saying that what counts is love.

"Merit" is never proportional to suffering. If it were, it
would lead to this nonsense: the less love there is, the more
merit there will be! Choose, like Socrates, an unbearable wife
whom it will certainly be impossible for you to love and,
through this long torture, go straight to heaven (the main
charm of which will be to be freed from this infernal presence!).

If merit were in proportion to deprivation, we should have
to take care not to love in order for it to remain "meritorious."

On the contrary! The more you do your work with joy (with
love), the more you accomplish every act of your life in faith,
gladness, hope, and attachment, the more Christian value your
life will have.

A work done with love has more "merit" than a work done
in boredom. A work one loves is more Christian than a work
one does not love. A service done to somebody one loves,
whom one has come to *love*, is more Christian than a service
done "for the love of God" to somebody one does not love.

Difficulty is first of all the sign that we do not love (and
therefore that we do not have any merit), but it may, however, incite us to love more.

Do not collect "merits" either . . . They are part of these
"strange virtues" like poverty, suffering, humility: "You think
you have it, and then, lo and behold, you have it no longer!"
As soon as we seek them, they slip away. By definition. You
act through self-love if you seek *your perfecting* in *your* suffering. Love—and suffer as you like. (Don't worry: you won't
miss out on it . . . if you *love*.)

Suffering does not necessarily lead to love, but love does
lead away, and soundly, to suffering.

*

God is love. There is, therefore, only one value, one valid
reference: love.

"God so *loved* the world . . . that he gave his Son." God asks but one thing from us: to love. God sent his Son in order to teach us one thing: how to love.

And what about the cross? And what about the call, "If any man would come after me, let him deny himself and take up his cross daily and follow me?" (Lk. 9, 23).

There is no contradiction. For under earthly conditions, to love *is* to suffer, immediately.

For to love is in fact to be raised towards another. And to exist, on earth, is tied up to such a heaviness, to such an instinct of retirement into one's self that this raising is a laceration.

The Son "made man," made earthly, made heaviness, "made sin," Saint Paul says, but still Son, that is, all *"élan,"* all return to the Father, this gives . . . the cross, the quartering.

All genuine love, in the same way, quarters us. Love—and suffering will be given to you in addition. Just as it has been said, in the name of the same divine logic: love, and poverty will be given to you in addition.

God wants to initiate us into a single thing: the happiness of loving. It is the only happiness he knows. It is the only one he can give us. This is what Christ tried—to the death—to make us understand.

Christ revealed love to us through his words, but first and above all through his life. This is the meaning of the cross. "When the eternal falls into the sea, it becomes a fish," a Japanese proverb says. When love fell into human nature, it became suffering. In God, love is a joyful mutual gift. In us, it is the renunciation of self-love.

And we know well that there is no means of loving without beginning to suffer, without having to control oneself, to forgive, to be disappointed, to be faithful even so, to believe beyond appearances, to believe in spite of appearances, to give credit sometimes "against all hope," to start again, always, painfully, to hope for everything, to wait for everything. ("Love believes all things, hopes all things, endures all things . . . ," untiringly). There is no profound affection which is not painful, excruciating. "When one gives oneself, one has oneself no longer."

The sin, the only sin (from which all the others derive) is to be incapable of loving.

Every man desires to know this exchange, this natural gift, this comprehension. And with his own strength, none is able to. Anatole France remarked that, in human affections, only the beginnings are delightful. This is why, he added, one always begins again!

When it lasts, it becomes painful. Why?

God, as for him, is what theologians call "subsistent relation." This means that his very being *is* to be "related" to, to be in relation with another. The Father is all motion of love towards the Son, as the Son is all motion of love towards the Father. God is all "*élan*," towards another . . .

Man, on the contrary, always tends to retire, to suffice unto himself, to prefer to manage by himself, to send all the others to the devil. And to send oneself to the devil which is not better.

Pride is not to have a good opinion of oneself (that's vanity). Pride, on the contrary, is to want to suffice unto oneself, to isolate oneself, to manage with one's own bad material, while hating oneself. To be at least independent since there is no means of being happy. Pride and despair cover the same resignation to stifle that thirst for happiness which would continue to draw us out so painfully towards others.

Pride, despair, resignation, withdrawal, excommunication: all words which mean the same thing. "It is my odor, it is bad but it is mine. I prefer to be unhappy by myself."

He who is damned is he who has succeeded in isolating himself completely.

Our individuality is the residue of our incapacity for giving. To love is to renounce this residue, this nucleus of security, of sterile but reassuring, anesthetizing immobility.

C. S. Lewis, who has written a book titled *The Problem of Pain*, expresses this by proposing the paradox of a certain "suffering" in heaven:

"As to its fellow-creatures, each soul, we suppose, will be

eternally engaged in giving away to all the rest that which it receives. And as to God, we must remember that the soul is but a hollow which God fills. Its union with God is, almost by definition, a continual self-abandonment—an opening, an un-veiling, a surrender of itself. . . . We need not suppose that the necessity for something analogous to self-conquest will ever be ended, or that eternal life will not also be eternal dy-ing. It is in this sense that, as there may be pleasures in hell (God shield us from them), there may be something not at all unlike pains in heaven (God grant us soon to taste them)."

This is not as paradoxical as it seems: those who love one another know well that, in the moment when one abandons oneself to another, when one surrenders oneself, there is something which gives the impression of both dying and being born.

When Christ became man, he began to conform his will painfully to that of another, as he had, from all eternity, con-formed it in heaven in joy. St. Paul tells us that "although he was a Son, he learned obedience" (Heb. 5, 8).

"Not my will, but thine": one cannot deny that there is here a "renunciation" of something, that Christ, "although he was a Son," had here to overcome this slight attachment to oneself which is inherent in human nature which he wanted to assume.

It is this overcoming, this renunciation, which Adam re-fused. He did not accept to believe that there was a possi-bility of saying: "Not my will, but thine" and being happy. He did not believe that suffering and love could coincide in joy. He did not accept to trust God in this way.

There is only one hell, but maybe you have experienced it already: it is the place where one no longer hopes for any-thing, where one no longer loves anybody, where one no longer expects anything from anybody, where one no longer trusts anybody.

To love is to tear oneself away from oneself in order to trust God and the others.

To begin loving others again is to be broken: but this is the virtue of hope.

Our children's angers already reveal quite well this satanic attraction well-known to men: "I'd rather die—and I hope all the others die too," the kid says to himself who stays in the corner while all the family calls him affectionately to come back into the circle of exchanges and joy.

One is not angry with him, he will not be punished, everything which life involves: nourishment, warmth, play . . . is on the side where others call him. He would have only to turn around. But he prefers to die.

This is temptation, the temptation of us all. It is the same infernal sin which will tempt us until the end of our days: the definitive settling down in the corner—where we will be left in peace, where in the end we will indeed suffer no longer, no longer hear any call, where the rending communication will indeed in the end be cut off, stifled. This is hell. To have lost the inclination to love—in order not to suffer any longer.

During their engagement, if they were asked, the lovers, of course, would come to deny this "wrench," this "crucifixion," this "renunciation" of love. But from the beginning of the honeymoon on they are led to discover the "Not my will, but thine" that their love will demand, every day, in order to grow.

It is the story of the young couple returned from their honeymoon and on whom the first morning at home dawns. Who is going to make the coffee? Who is going to get up first, there, disagreeably, in the cold, to go make the coffee for the other?

"At home it is always mother who makes coffee," the young man thinks. "If they no longer do that, what will they do?", he adds at once, moved by this fugitive evocation of his mother and looking with concern at the apathy of this "very nice but slightly lymphatic girl." It is important to develop good habits from the very first day, he was told. This is the moment. He wraps himself up in his covers and presents to his companion a rounded and peremptory back.

"He said he would give anything for me," the young woman is thinking all the while. "He said he would go to the end of the world. And the first effort, the first task, I am the one who can do it. What a disillusion! What a twirp! They are all the same. I'm not going to move."

Each one feels that to get up would be to capitulate on the whole line, to put oneself at the mercy of the other. And they love each other . . . but not as much as that.

Whereas if he had done it at once, on his own, in the joyous impulse of thinking of the other's welfare rather than of his own, he who would have gotten up would have felt that he was so much the richer, so much the better provided for, that he had so much good fortune in being able to rejoice and gratify the other, . . . that he would have pitied the other so poor, so stuck, so encumbered with himself.

The problem for him would have become: How to carry this tray with enough discretion, enough good humor, enough tactfulness and inadvertence in order not to humiliate the other with this coffee!

Love decenters and delivers. But one must begin by plunging. By jumping out of the warm and comfortable bed. He who loses his life saves it. But one must first accept "losing." One has to go through this painful wrench.

To go from selfishness to love, is nearly as violent as an atomic disintegration. It resembles it.

What makes the integrity of the atom is that it is a closed system where electrons turn eternally, around *their* nucleus.

Everything blows up, everything moves, everything comes to life when an electron, through an extraordinary dynamism, wrenches itself free from this infernal round, gets interested in a nucleus which is not his own, enters the circuit of another.

When we start to love, that is to say to prefer the will of someone other than ourselves to ours, it is a psychological upheaval of the same kind. But eternal life is at this price. For it *is* love.

And there also is joy. "I came (not that they may suffer but) that they may have my joy fulfilled in themselves" Christ says before ascending Calvary.

This life, this joy—we will only reach them through cracking. No transfiguration without a previous disfiguration. You are promised a new face (transfiguration) but meanwhile . . . you have first to lose face. And nobody does that with pleasure.

God risks everything. To open oneself to God is to take the leap of death.

Jesus came to go about on earth, giving himself to everybody, letting everybody approach him, absorb him, devour him: being completely available—to anybody.

The epistle already quoted (Mass of the Good Shepherd) says of him: he let himself be maltreated; he did not say a word; he surrendered himself without threats to the hands of those who judged him unjustly.

Jesus did not seek the cross (he hated it: my Father, if it be possible, let this cup pass from me . . . My soul is very sorrowful, even to death . . .) but he has been faithful in all its consequences to the *Yes* he came to pronounce, he came to incarnate in order to save us.

We have said *Yes* by our baptism, we have said *Yes* by our marriage, we repeat *Yes* when we participate in the celebration of the Mass.

And we know it is a joy and a quartering. The cross of Christ is this fidelity—and not an asceticism which would be more Greek or Hindu than Christian. "You did not want sacrifices or holocausts but you gave me a body. And I said: 'here I am.'" Christ became man in order to love as a man—through suffering.

Do not imagine Jesus "overwhelmed under the weight of the Father's anger!" He is all uplifted, on the contrary, by the thought of the Father, by his constant presence near him. "You will leave me alone" he says to the apostles "yet I am not alone, for the Father is with me" (Jn. 16, 32). When he is exhausted, it is thinking of the Father that gives him courage, peace, and certitude again.

Do not imagine God "who avenges himself" on an innocent for the offense of the guilty. But a Son who puts all his fervor in loving his Father.

Jesus, on the cross, does nothing else than in heaven: he

loves. "When he was crucified, Christ merely accompished on this earth, in his distant provinces, amidst the tumult of the elements, what he unceasingly does in his house, in glory and in joy."

*

This love, Christ communicates to us. Christ, become "life-giving spirit" through his resurrection, capable of incorporating into himself every creature, gives us the capacity of loving like him.

There is a grace of conformity to and union with Christ which is proposed to each man, and which works in him to lead him to love, to suffer, to detach himself, to entrust himself.

Rejoice: you do not suffer, above all, because you have sinned, but because Christ suffered, and because you resemble him. You will not die because Adam sinned, but because Christ died and obtained that your life and your death become like his: filial and redeeming.

The communion of saints allows us to believe that the addition of suffering which strikes what remains innocent in us only exists to be used for the redemption of those who have received less. "To suffer too much is a form of expiation."

God is not paternalist! He is a Father. He does not content himself with giving, he gives us the capacity of giving in our turn. "Beloved, Christ also suffered for you, leaving you an example, that you should follow in his steps . . ." (1 Pet. 2, 21).

✦ V ✦

THE EVIL IN THIS WORLD

The root of suffering, the root of evil, we have seen, is human imperfection. Adam sinned not because he was weak but because he was man.

Necessary, inevitable imperfection. To want only perfection is to annihilate the creation. If God creates, he has to create something created, that is to say, imperfect, something which is distinct from him.

The world is unfinished, revelation tells us. Adam and Eve had the mission of "cultivating the Garden," of improving paradise! For this unfinished world can be completed and God invites us to work at it with him.

The infinite perfectibility is what corresponds in the creature to the infinite perfection of God. It is the spring of our hope, an inexhaustible reason for our rejoicing.

For this natural imperfection becomes a real evil, a true suffering, only if we refuse to feed it and to nourish it at the source of the communicated Perfection, if we pretend to suffice unto ourselves.

To want to be autonomous is for us to refuse our fulfillment in God. It is to begin Adam's sin over again. It is to leave the life of the Vine for the mortal tranquillity of the dry branch.

Evil can be explained because God trusted man: God made the creature creative. The freedom of man is genuine. Man is capable of initiative. He creates new things in the world, and therefore evil; if he does not complete the world, he damages it. And the whole of humanity will suffer collectively the consequences, happy or not, of his choice!

The world was created good.

Be careful: this does not mean orderly, harmonious, but only capable of being ordered, of being organized.

*

Does God remain impassive and, as it were, neutral before the use of freedom? Does he look "from the height of heaven" at our massacres, as we would look at the eddies of an ants' nest, waiting for the end "to judge the living and the dead"? To imagine God in this way is to make oneself liable to no longer believing in him (for how could one bear such a terrible image of love?), or to split one's life into two parts, so to speak: into one part which thinks of God while forgetting all the rest, and into a second part which thinks of all the rest, while trying to forget God. To imagine God in such a way is never to look at heaven and earth at the same time.

But this is obviously wrong. God wanted man to be free, God allowed this dreadful risk, only because he felt powerful enough to compete with man in intervention. To compensate by his initiatives of love all the evil that man could imagine.

A solemn dialogue has begun between God and the creature. God says, You will do what you want, but I notify you that every time I will invent something to triumph over your evil. I will never abandon you. I will make of each of your faults fortunate faults. I will unceasingly offer you marvellous reparations for your ravages ("O God who created man in grandeur, and restored him in a still more admirable way . . ."). Everything will be more beautiful than if you had not sinned. From your shame and your pain, I, God, draw a virtue which would not have existed if you had not made a slip. Your famous original sin is the origin, much more than of your troubles, of the wonders which I, God, invent to make it good. Adam misused his freedom? *Felix culpa*: the Word became flesh and dwelt among us. Eve lost us? I invented Mary. Each of you is tormented by desires for the forbidden fruit? Each one will be tempted and devoured by the thirst for the living God. Be confident: I have overcome evil.

None of your sins is decisive. There will always be my forgiveness and our reparation. No life is a failure. I will offer you until the end to begin it over again in a more wonderful way and to become a new creature (2 Cor. 5, 17). You are dead? I will raise you up.

The cross is the conclusion of this dialogue between evil and good, begun in the earthly paradise—a concise, tragic, prodigious dialogue in which good has the last word: "Into your hands, O Lord . . ." The creature has returned to the Creator.

*

It is in this light that the beatitudes are to be understood, the triumphal song of the victory of God in the midst of all human sufferings.

Blessed are those who mourn, those who thirst, those who hunger . . . Blessed are those who are incapable of being happy. Blessed are those who know that they will never be happy by themselves, alone. Blessed are those who need another, blessed are those who need all the others in order to be happy.

First, those who suffer are the true witnesses of the human condition. They proclaim that the world is sick, that human life is impossible. Usually one becomes aware of it only in catastrophes, in those most normal, most foreseeable, most certain events which we call catastrophes. Yes indeed, in accidents, mourning, illness, war, everybody thinks it obvious that life is too hard, too unjust, too sorrowful, too painful. But our big mistake is not to know it beforehand. The great error in face of an illness, an accident, is to believe that evil is suddenly appearing in an innocent and happy life.

Evil is something permanent, a lot worse when it is admitted, when one is used to it than when it appears under a new and striking form. Our weakness of character, our selfishness, the habitual misfortune of others, we have accepted once for all. Habitual injustice seems just, habitual sin seems benign, habitual catastrophe seems normal: "They drink sin like water, they eat up the poor like bread."

Blessed are those who suffer! Blessed, by comparison, those who are revolted and tormented by injustice.

We usually live in a monstrous unconsciousness. We have settled down into an incredible apathy. One finds it natural . . . that the rich stuff themselves while some people die of hunger (it is even thought very bad taste to remember it, sometimes, at table), that intelligent children are deprived of studies while dunces, if they come from a well-to-do milieu, overcrowd classes they only keep up with by means of private lessons. How many parasites, of this kind, in a "good college"? And how many wasted unemployed gifts in other milieux because of the lack of money, of time, of support. "Studies do not cost anything?" "There are scholarships?" And what about the rest? And what about the food which no income compensates for as soon as a child studies? And what about decent clothes in order to rub elbows with these other children better provided for, better dressed, better fed, better rested, better entertained, without being scorned?

The poor earn little, study little, aim at little. And those who nonetheless try to get out of the rut are very often considered dangerous people, radicals, social misfits. It is preferable that they stagnate. The rich resign themselves heroically to the resignation of the poor!

Those who suffer are altered. Whatever the reason, it is already something to have one foot out of this ignoble security. Those who suffer are the witnesses in the world of the crying need for God.

*

The worst evil is not to know that one is hurt, the worst evil is not to know that one is in evil, the worst evil is not to know that one *is* evil!

The worst punishment of God would be to let us sink, without the least anxiety, into this "happiness," made up of insensitiveness and callousness, which is the very image and as it were the sacrament of hell.

Suffering reminds us that we are not made for this world of sin, that we are not of the world, that the world must be changed, modified, upset—converted. C. S. Lewis says that suffering "plants the flag of truth within the fortress of a rebel soul."

Moral theologians sometimes pose the following question: Which is the greater moral evil, for a person to commit sin while knowing that his action is a sin, or to commit sin while thinking that he is in the right?

To prefer ignorance in order to preserve one's innocence is an absurdity. Say at once that your ideal is to become more and more stupid! (And by the way, do not have too many illusions about the innocence of this attitude. It must be with this kind of "good intentions" that the way to hell is paved.)

For those who know, there is at least a little hope that they may change. To see clearly is the first step towards conversion, a first invitation of God to set oneself in motion.

God, thus, from time to time, seems to want to accelerate this progress towards him for which we prove to be in so little a hurry. As for him, he waits for us with such impatience . . . and we go, generally, with feet of lead.

Blessed are those who are persecuted: for they are taken, grasped by God—who knew that at bottom they did not refuse as much as they seemed to, and who was exhausted with waiting for them.

Blessed are those who mourn . . . If you are asked, after a great trial, "Would you want to go through it again?", it is obvious that you will answer: "Never." But if you are asked, "Would you like not to have gone through it?", and "Are you going to behave exactly as before?" —then you will begin to measure all that these hours of bitterness and anxiety brought to you and you will give thanks. If it has cured you of a blindness, will you not admit that suffering is a light?

Suffering transforms, matures, and instructs. Suffering increases our capacities of love and understanding. All suffering makes us have something in common with any of those who suffer. It is a power of communion.

Undoubtedly, suffering sometimes hardens us. It does not necessarily bring us closer to *virtue*. But it always brings us closer to truth.

Suffering and death are the only unavoidable obstacles which compel the most mediocre man to call himself into question, to detach himself from his existence, and to ask himself what would permit him to transcend it.

What neither love, nor prayer, nor poetry, nor art could do for most people, only death and suffering are capable of demanding.

But maybe the day will come when love, art, and prayer will have enough power over us so that we might be exempt from suffering and death.

*

But, you will say, what about ignorant people? People incapable of knowing, of feeling all that? What about mental defectives? What about babies? How can we accept that God allows the suffering of babies?

Well, suppose first of all that no spiritual being can be put in possession of his eternal destiny without making an act of choice. Then, of two babies, one filled with milk, pink and content, the other grown pale, struck by some disease, participating in his flesh in some universal misfortune, which baby seems to you more oriented towards the kingdom, which seems to you more ready to "pass away," to say, in whatever way, "Into your hands, Lord, I commit my spirit"?

Warned in his body, and through it in his as yet infirm conscience, he is prepared, for the moment when death will suddenly make him adult, to respond to the invitation of the Lord: Come to me, all of you who are heavy-laden . . .

The blessing of hospitals, of people condemned to death, of sanitoriums, of all these places where one suffers, is that there people can be found who know that they need help, who no longer pretend to have no need of God or of anyone, who are freed from this exhausting comedy.

Children already pretend to be grown-ups, pretend to be happy all alone. With children already, as soon as they grow a little, relationships are altered, openness becomes difficult. They try to suffice unto themselves. They try out original sin, slowly they train themselves for it.

Only somebody true, somebody made true through suffering, knows how to accept the most beautiful thing in the world which a human being can give to another: compassion —this sharing—this communion.

"I was hungry and you gave me food, I was a stranger and you welcomed me, I was in prison and you came to me . . ." (Mt. 25). This is the greatest kind of exchange, the most "divine" relationship which can be established between two people.

Thus suffering initiates us, forewarns us, in the midst of the unconsciousness of the healthy. The unfortunate are confidants of God, they are invited to become like God who suffers from the evil of this world and who loves enough to suffer from it.

The beatitudes are a description of divine behavior, an evocation of the atmosphere of the kingdom. "Blessed are the poor, those who are persecuted . . . for theirs is the kingdom of heaven." They will feel at home there. They are made for the kingdom. They already have its style, its mark, its manners. They are naturalized in advance.

God is someone whose heart is sensitive to every distress. Blessed are the merciful—because God is merciful. God, the prophets say, has "entrails of mercy." God is a man of heart, Péguy used to say. Those who suffer share the feelings of God, share his way of seeing the world.

*

That amounts to saying that God is vulnerable.

The "impassiveness" of God is perhaps a philosophical necessity. But the "God of Jesus Christ" . . . *suffers*. The Father of the crucified . . . *suffers*. And the Shepherd anxious about his lost sheep, running after them in brambles and thickets, . . . *suffers*.

The smug, comfortable happiness, which a certain rational way of speaking of God suggests, repels us and rightly so. It is not in that way that God has spoken of God. We feel instinctively that the revelation of God takes place at the level of the greatest suffering.

How can one imagine a God preserved, steeped in his happiness, impassive in his clouds . . . whereas, when he manifested himself, he came—to suffer, to die? When God presented himself to us "in the days of his flesh," if he chose poverty, humility, and finally condemnation, judgment, abandonment, and failure . . . it is because these were the human values the most capable of translating into our language what God is.

*

The most precious image we have of God is that of a severely wounded person who is dying. God wanted us to find him again and to venerate him in the poor, the wounded, the insane. He established between him and us a mysterious solidarity which allows his sufferings to become ours, as ours were his.

But let us be careful, once more, that the suffering which is thus made sacred, is the suffering of the Redeemer, a suffering born of love, full of love.

Christ is not only the being who suffers the most, he is above all the one who saves the most. He came to "save what was lost." We should not have the mystique of perdition, the obsession of suffering, but the obsession of salvation.

If any person who suffers is sacred to us, because of him whom he resembles, any person who nurses, who helps someone to his feet, who consoles or heals, is even more completely the image of Christ.

Christ revealed that evil can be overcome, that evil can be redeemed, that there is a victory of love over death and suffering, and that there exists a redemption after the worst falls. Then indeed, our respect and our devotion to the sinners and to the sick should be the sacrament, the announcement, the assurance of the redemption. Through our poor words, through our poor care, through our poor love, another love is manifested. The love and compassion of Christ for the sick, the gestures of Christ washing the eyes of the blind, anointing the ears of the deaf, purifying the body of the lepers, weeping with compassion over Lazarus! It is true that you can be healed, it is true that you can be saved, it is true that you can still be loved, even when you are sick, when you are fallen, when you are ruined! The sinner, the insane, the condemned would be exposed to the worst temptation, despair, if the kindness, the tenderness, the respect of those who claim to belong to Christ did not dispose them little by little to believe that the Father, too, loves them, that if they are already so much loved, understood, pitied on this earth, they are much more so in heaven, and that the Father keeps them in sight with the same infinite compassion, the same tenderness, the same admiration and pride, with which he contemplated his Son dying on the cross.

No, the final victory over evil is neither anesthetics, nor even healing, but love which cures us of ourselves.

*

There is something harder than to suffer: it is to see those we love suffer and not be able to do anything to relieve them.

Often there is in this an unconscious selfishness. We refuse their suffering because we are not capable of seeing them suffer. We would accept this trial if it were to happen to us, and we know well the good we would get from it. But this good, we do not want for those we love, for it is too painful for us to see them acquiring it.

Let us be careful, above all when it is a question of someone close to us, not to substitute for his true happiness the idea we have of the way he should be happy.

I remember a bad night I once spent with two friends. They were on a camping trip, and I arrived unexpectedly to spend the night. The tent had only two cots; my friends had just gone to bed. I would have been perfectly rested the following morning if I could only have lain on the ground, between them, in my sleeping-bag. But they felt remorse! And they wanted by all means for me to "share" the comfort of one of their cots. I proved to them in vain that I would be much better on the ground than on half a cot . . . but their scruples demanded that I not be on the ground, and I had to resign myself to a long "comfortable" insomnia in order to correspond to the idea they had of my needs and of the demands of hospitality.

On every level and for much more serious things, we have this tendency to project around us our need of unconcern and security.

When someone we love suffers, we should say to ourselves, God is more confident in him than I, God is more ambitious for him than I, God loves him more profoundly, more audaciously than I, God does not content himself, for him, with a quiet little happiness like that which I, in my mediocre way, imagined.

Our clumsy revolt, our clumsy displays in order to protect those we love from what we believe to be their misfortune, are generally more harmful than what we are so much afraid of.

Pity is easily egoistic. Read Graham Greene's *The Heart of the Matter* and you will see the catastrophe to which the incapacity to see or to make those one loves suffer can lead.

To want to please "everybody and his uncle" is the surest means of displeasing both. Not to want to make anyone suffer is often to make everyone suffer.

But above all, the temptation which lies in wait for pity is despair: it is to deny any redemptive value to suffering, and therefore to revolt against life, against the cross, against God.

God loves infinitely more than we and yet, he sees, he makes or lets suffer those whom he loves. Can't we trust him for that which goes beyond our power and our rights?

Pity will either make suffering intolerable to us by revolt and despair, or else, thanks to faith in the redemption of Christ and in our prayer, it will become humble compassion, a silent Veronica.

*

There is only one way not to let ourselves be scandalized by the vision of evil triumphing everywhere and of suffering torturing those dearest to us. It is to take refuge in the suffering Christ.

Only he who created the world is capable of bearing the sin of the world. Only he can bear the cross, who died on the cross.

We should not flee from the sight of the suffering of others, but we should not let ourselves be overburdened by it in trying to bear it alone. We would end up, as many who are scandalized of the existence of evil, by extending still further its ravages.

Let us take refuge at the feet of Christ crucified and let us hear him say, "Be of good cheer, I have overcome the world," I found the means of assuming all this suffering, I know how to bear all this evil. You would not be able to do it. You would succumb under your burden. Come, take mine. It is the only one tolerable for you. Take my yoke. This one is light. Because in taking it you take me at the same time, it is my life, my prayer, my love, and my joy. "I give you my peace." — "It is no longer I who live," St. Paul said; it is no longer I who labor, it is no longer I who suffer, "but Christ who lives in me." "I am crucified . . . with Christ."

And Christ, like us, balks at the cross: "What shall I say? 'Father, save me from this hour?'" But *he* is capable of correcting himself at once and of adding: " 'No, for this purpose I have come to this hour. Father, glorify thy name.' Then a voice came from heaven, 'I have glorified it and I will glorify it again'" (Jn. 12, 27–28).

At the beginning of each Mass, we are invited to this surmounting, to this trust: Why are you sad, my soul, why are you troubled? —Hope in God. I will praise him again: My Saviour and my God!

We must efface ourselves, we must suffer in second place, we must follow . . . like Simon of Cyrene. We must follow without thinking in the footsteps of another who knows where he is going. We must allow to grow in ourselves someone who will know how to do what we were incapable of doing: to trust, to abandon ourselves, to commit ourselves to the Father. Then our way of the cross will become like his a way of love and joy.

We should not celebrate the Mass of the suffering of the world but serve it.

Christ has taken care of celebrating it. We just have to respond, to correspond from time to time, to make little gestures, one after the other: to bring a little wine, to pour a little water, to carry the Book, to pronounce short responses —to communicate.

We must communicate—receive Christ's life—in order to become like Christ, to be able, in our turn, to let ourselves be judged, condemned, insulted . . . without opening our mouth.

We complete, in our flesh what is lacking in Christ's sufferings. But it is indeed because he, first, completed forever what is lacking so dreadfully in ours.

*

"Come to me, all who labor and are heavy laden . . . and learn from me; for I am gentle and lowly in heart . . ." It is from him, in him, that we will learn this divine gentleness which consists in being tenacious, persevering, untiringly faithful, loving in failure, loving in trial. It is from him, in him, that we will learn to be humble in heart—to continue humbly to love him who refuses our affection, because we have the confidence that Christ can reach a person when we only succeed in jostling or in shattering him more.

Humble in heart: Christ did not wait for us to have changed to offer us his love. But because he loved us "first," we have a chance to change. To finally be willing to love him a little too. To accept his invitations. To go to the rendezvous he gives us. To respond to his humble call.

*

To enter into the mystery of suffering is to trust the paternal omnipotence of God. It means to learn to say "Father!", like Jesus, from the depth of the most excruciating anxiety: Father, I know that you hear me always.

To enter into the mystery of suffering, is to believe, whatever may happen to us, that it is a new call to confide in God's tenderness.

Blessed are those who mourn: blessed are those who, in the worst bitterness, are audacious enough to believe in the tender solicitude of the Father, who are audacious enough to think themselves blessed and not "punished," encouraged, awaited—a cause for joy: "This is my beloved son, with whom I am well pleased."

The heavenly beatitude will be the evocation of a competition in audacity! See how I dared to love! See how far I dared not to doubt the Lord! See how far I dared to see in my way of the cross a way of joy.

Our feeling towards Jesus should first of all be to rejoice that a Son could love his Father in this way. ". . . So that the world may know that I love the Father."

And we will be in our turn sons, daughters, after him and like him, inasmuch as we will know, likewise, how to trust the Father.

What depth of evil, of sin, of humiliation, of injustice, of depression, of failure, and of tiredness will we be able to bear without ceasing to say, —We have believed in love. We believe in love. Through all this, Lord, we have dared to believe in love.

This is what we should be able to say when we come to heaven. This is what we should say, every day, when we come to mass, which is the beginning of heaven.

And he answers us, and he repeats to us, every day, as to his disciples: Be of good cheer, I have overcome the world, I have overcome all this evil. I *am* this suffering, this cross, this excruciating love. Do not be afraid.

In Christ, with Christ, suffering has become a means of communion and a place of redemption.

The evil of misfortune and the evil of crime, the suffering of the victim and the moral poverty of the guilty, all this can and should find its redemption through the generous love of those who acknowledge their solidarity with it.

What the world lacks in order to respond to the problem of

evil, is not clever arguments, it is redeemers in sufficient number!

Look at a big city, at these innumerable human cells, these windows, these lights, at night, which signal lives and send a call; do you believe in a love vigilant enough and generous enough to justify all these existences, to despair of none of them, to consider all of them as infinitely precious and invite them untiringly to believe, to awaken, to open up to this blessed certitude of being loved beyond all miseries?

As for us, Christians, we believe that "our Redeemer is living," and that through us, in us, with us, he reaches the farthest parts of the world.

Evil is not yet defeated, but, like the redemption, the solution to the problem of evil is at work in the heart of each of us.

There would not be anything worse than to give, abstractly, a satisfying and premature solution for it.

Indifference, resignation, or ignorance of evil makes selfish and inert people; but anxiety about the living evil which seems to triumph in the world makes redeemers.

As long as the last saint has not said his last prayer, it is not yet sure that all men will not be saved.

It could be that by dint of prayer, struggle, suffering, and failure, the saints ceaselessly atone for the faults of their vanquishers and that on the day when the redemption will burst forth, we will see with wonder that the world has been redeemed, that some hearts of fire and faith have succeeded in making good all this evil which had so often overburdened, embittered, discouraged us.

VI

THE PRINCE OF THIS WORLD

"They did not understand this saying, and it was concealed from them, that they should not perceive it; and they were afraid to ask him about this saying" (Lk. 9, 45). This is the way, the Gospel tells us, the apostles received the first confidence of Christ about his coming passion. Twenty centuries later our reaction is the same. In us also, if we are sincere, the thought of the passion of the Lord provokes the same response of stupefaction, uneasiness, and painful incomprehension. Now, frankly, who among us has the feeling that his own sins deserve such a punishment, who feels guilty enough to believe that his faults demand such a redemption? Let us dare to go further and ask: Who considers his own life—the life of a person who has been saved, of a redeemed, baptized person —worth the terrible price it cost? Who truly believes that the passion is justified, who is not secretly dismayed, stupefied, bewildered by the weight of this tragedy when he considers that it is his soul that is the stake, the object of it all?

To be sure, these questions sound like a blasphemy of ingratitude, but is not the most genuine prayer to recognize the whole extent of our misery and to say to God that it is not sufficient that he save us, but that he must also reveal, to most of us, the necessity and the benefit of it.

In fact, all this comes from the fact that we have lost the sense of sin, the sense of its seriousness, of its reality, of its vitality in us and around us. We no longer know how powerful evil is, we no longer know that evil is somebody, somebody wicked and strong, infinitely more clever, more malicious,

more intelligent than we: and that we are but "weak crea-
tures of flesh swept away in the revolt of somebody stronger
than we." We no longer believe in sin, or in Satan, and this is
why we also no longer believe in God, or in the redemption,
or in joy.

We have so well camouflaged evil in our lives, our consciences are so elastic, our confessions so impersonal, we have
got so used to calling evil good and good evil, we are so skilled
in respecting appearances and doing evil without suffering the
consequences, that, when we are suddenly confronted with all
the blood, all the suffering, all the love which burst out in the
passion of Christ, we are astounded, and we wonder whether
he really meant to do all of this for us.

And yet, one has but to read the Gospel to see that Jesus,
from the very beginning of his ministry, encounters an un-
believable power of evil which he calls the Prince of this
World. Everywhere he denounces him, he pursues him, he
dethrones him. And when the latter, after having failed to
make him to receive his kingdom from his hands, throws
against him all his forces, all those whom he has in his power,
all the men who are devoted and subject to him, this incredible thing is revealed, that it was in fact the whole world,
the Jews and the Romans, the rich and the poor, the priests
and the laymen, the pontiffs and the bad thief. Yes, he was
in fact the Prince of this World, and Jesus had indeed told
us so. Here we see evil, the extent and dimension of the
power of evil in the world.

Do you think that the people who heard Jesus without believing him, who rejected, condemned, and crucified him,
were so much more wicked than we?

No indeed! They did it, as we do it, with all kinds of good
reasons, providing themselves with a good conscience, led by
a current of opinion (like us, when we do not believe in the
devil), approved of by their milieu, moved by fear or interest,
maneuvered by an occult Power. They did it exactly as we do:
without knowing what they were doing. They served the devil,
and they did not know it.

The church believes in the devil. It baptizes children (and

you became Christian only because you solemnly renounced Satan); it multiplies exorcisms; it blesses every object which is presented to it in order to consecrate it to God. Not because it claims that we are all possessed by the devil, but because it knows the structures of sin in which we are all caught, entwined, smothered, since we came into the world.

God loves and gives the capacity of loving, God unites and reassembles. He wanted, since the beginning, for husband and wife to be only one flesh, indissoluble. Jesus came in order to unite in one Body the children of God who are scattered.

But the devil divides and separates. Remember how Adam, after having welcomed Eve with an acclamation of joy, —"This at last is bone of my bones and flesh of my flesh"—, disassociated himself from her in an ugly way, as soon as he had sinned and submitted himself to the influence of the devil. He shifted upon her the responsibility of his fault, as all spouses do in domestic quarrels: "The woman whom thou gavest to be with me, she gave me fruit of the tree!"

It is Satan who divides spouses, who divides parents from children (Noah and his sons), brother from brother (Cain and Abel), men among themselves. The present world, tragically divided, divorced, incapable of love and agreement is a striking manifestation of the influence of Satan.

Even for those who do not believe in Christ, even for those who do not believe in the Church, it seems to me that there exists an obvious proof of the existence of the devil: the presence and the action of evil in the world so surpass the capacity, the wickedness of the men who accomplish it. There is in the activity of evil in the world something organized, willed, prodigiously clever which denounces its author.

Men generally sin through stupidity: "They do not know what they are doing!", and they discover, afterwards, that they did not want what they have done.

But the devil is remarkably intelligent. He is lucid, Lucifer!

Think of the concentration camps: the cruelty of the torturers, their ingenuity in the debasement of their victims, there reached a point which verges on genius. And yet, take them away from this environment, from this implacable organization, see them outside of it, or some years later, and they have become men like others. The torturers are often good husbands, tender fathers, obliging and friendly neighbors. They were merely trapped in an infernal mesh which dragged them mercilessly beyond the evil which they were personally capable of committing.

Take more banal and apparently innocent structures: the distinctions of class, of language, of color, of race, of nationality. Suppose normal, good, human, reasonable men: it suffices that someone differ from them by the color of his skin, his language, a mere frontier beyond which he was born, and he becomes for them the hereditary enemy, the irreconcilable adversary.

See the morality in business: how many professions where it is impossible to be honest, where everything is negotiated through commissions and bribes, recommendations and the traffic of influence. Each of those involved complains of it individually, but the structure is such that nobody can free himself from it.

Let us place ourselves on the world-wide scale: famine combined with overproduction. One third of the world stuffs itself and has to be careful about its figure (and it is as if by chance our world, the Christian world), and the other two thirds suffer from hunger and show signs of deficiency, threats of exhaustion.

And this is not caused by wickedness, hatred, oppression. It is the result of forces which escape individuals; the latter are kept in unconsciousness, they feel powerless to react, they are caught in a system which surpasses them, they are the victims of a diabolical force which utilizes them in its plans.

How is it possible to spend billions to send rockets into space while so many people on earth lack the necessities of life? There is competition to colonize the moon, to conquer and lay out Mars, while one has not yet managed to humanize our planet.

The expenses for armament would be sufficient to double at once the income of all the underdeveloped countries. The price of only one Russian or American super-bomber would make it possible to heal leprosy in the whole world, and the expenses of the last World War would have covered the building of comfortable houses for each family in our hemisphere.

There is something worse: humanity is beginning to think calmly of the possibility of an atomic war. Shelters are built, chances of survival are calculated, one organizes in anticipation of it, one threatens one another daily with it, and one dares to use it as an argument in international discussions.

Do you not discover in this the influence of him who, the first in the history of the world, preferred his ruin and annihilation to the act of faith and love which was asked of him? Do you not feel in this cold hardness with which humanity considers its suicide, something mad, blind, inhumanly proud which reminds us of the first universal catastrophe, the first revolt, the first insurrection?

Undoubtedly, there are some who believe too much in the devil, and they risk letting themselves be fascinated by him, and distracted from God and from themselves by the obsession of his influence. It is infinitely more important to believe in God than to believe in the devil, and it is very important to know that God haunts us and tempts us infinitely more for the good than the devil for the evil. But it is still more dangerous to negate, to ignore the devil: it is the best way to serve him as a plaything.

Do you believe in the devil? Have you observed him at work, in you and around you? Have you never felt the terrible power of evil which works upon us and which, at certain times, bursts into our life? Have you never been amazed at what you have become capable of, at what you have managed to think of, to wish, to imagine, to do?

Oh! the devil does not appear to us, it is useless; a little money, a little flesh, a little honor is enough for him to have us in his power.

Indeed, it is not necessary to know a man very long to find the hole in his shell, the worm in the fruit, the vice or the shame which he hides, the blood, his or that of the others, with which he pays his success and has signed his contract. Undoubtedly, we all go around with a mask, we all pretend to be good, respectable, honest, worthy, serious, but inside, all are full of ruins, doubts, and longings. The youngest still doubt it, but the others know it or learn it, beginning with the oldest. Jesus, who knew what was in man, did not trust men. He told us how he judged us: "you who are evil," and this is a word of reality, a refreshing word in the immense hypocrisy which kills us: we are never closer to forgiveness and salvation than when we recognize ourselves as sinners. And it is Jesus who said this terrible word: "I am the door of the sheep. All who came before me are thieves and robbers." We, thieves and robbers? And when Jesus tore off the masks of the most indignant of his listeners, when he told them in front of all: "Let him who is without sin among you be the first to throw a stone at her," the crowd saw with stupefaction how misleading were appearances and what man was in reality. Indeed, the life of a man seen from the inside is not beautiful: all the evil we have done knowingly, all the evil we have done unknowingly—but with how many precautions to hide it from ourselves. All the ugly motives for our doing good: it is always our vices which give the best energy to our virtues, and we never do good so actively as when we have a bad reason for doing it. All the good and beautiful causes for which we have done evil, nourishing our monsters unstintingly in the darkness, with our face raised towards the stars.

And above all, our dreadful inner misery, our dreadful indifference to the suffering of others, not to mention the mad joy about the harm which happens to them. Our irresistible need for self-affirmation, for self-assertion, which is the stimulus of all our words, of all our gestures. Our insensitivity, our ingratitude before the beauty of the world and the goodness of life; and above all, our terrible poverty of faith, love, hope, and charity. Our inconceivable hostility against God: the harshness with which we criticize everything he does, revolt against all that he sends us, are afraid of all that he prepares, are disheartened in all that happens to us. Our resolution to sin, our fundamental determination to prefer ourselves, to suffice unto ourselves, to prefer to be unhappy alone than happy with him, thanks to him.

Aren't you like this yourself? Aren't you alarmed at being like this, so much worse than you ever wanted? Don't you see that you, too, are tied up by a "mighty one" who does his work and his will in you, and from whom you must at last be delivered by a "Mightier One"?

It is only when you know yourself in this way, it is only when you judge yourself that you begin to imagine, to desire what the redemption would accomplish, and cry out to the Redeemer. It is only when you recognize with certainty that you will never manage by yourself, that you will never change, you will never free yourself by yourself, that you must become other, that you must become another, that you must live another life, that somebody else must give you his life, it is only then that you begin to open yourself to the joy of the redemption.

I think that many of us only began to understand and to accept the passion, the redemption, after the revelation of the war and of the concentration camps. Before the war, before the two wars (before the terrible revelation that the same passion for evil dwelt in the hearts of our contemporaries), the scene of the outrages, Jesus at the pillar, Jesus crowned with thorns, Jesus stripped of his garments, Jesus crucified, all these were for us scenes of another age, violent variegations, stories of another time. But after what we saw, after what our friends told us, after what our parents and relatives suffered, the Gospel suddenly came to life again for many of us. We again felt the Stranger, the Prince of Darkness, the Evil One, the Tempter with his despair working and prowling around us. We felt so much evil around us and so great a weakness and powerlessness within us. When we thought of our brothers, of our friends who were there, our hearts were no doubt exasperated with pity and anger. But what a great joy, too, to think that Jesus had lived, had suffered all that. What immense relief we felt in thinking that his love had accompanied them, had preceded them that far. At one moment or another, they must have thought of it, they must have met him, they must have recognized themselves in it. At any one of the stations of their own way of the cross, they

must have known which love they had suddenly met and re-
joined. When they were stripped of their garments, they perhaps understood at this moment, for the first time, why Jesus
had consented to be stripped of his garments, they exchanged
a look with him, they understood one another and recognized
one another. When they were beaten, humiliated, perhaps
the thought of him whom they had become crossed their
mind for an instant, they understood why Jesus had wanted
to be insulted and scourged, they understood what humble,
silent, faithful love had waited for them there for centuries.
When they fell from exhaustion, in those death marches, they
found out that their falls were the repetition of other falls
and that they were entering a wonderful fraternity. Beyond
time and place, someone had thought of them, someone had
followed them, someone had suffered everything in order to
be there with them, so that when everybody had abandoned
them, when our love was no longer able to protect them or to
help them, they might still have a friend, a companion in
chains and on the cross, and that the purest, the noblest, the
tenderest, and the most comforting image of what they had
become could come to meet them. What a joy to think that
our parents and our friends, at some moment, thought this,
experienced this, and that, at the limit of human strength,
in oppression and fear, they were not alone, they found this
friend, they met this love in proportion with their distress,
and accepted this salvation. They found the "Mightier One"
who delivers from all chains, and, because they saw and understood their misery, they welcomed this love.

For us too, it is only when we despair of ourselves, of our
illusory safety, of our superficial virtues, it is only when we
recognize ourselves as sinners, when we know that, in spite
of appearances, we are undermined by dangers and weaknesses
which can from one moment to the next burst out and place
us in the same ranks as those whom we now hate or pity, it is
only then that we open ourselves to the salvation which comes
from another, that we can open ourselves to the joy of being
loved to this extent, of being forgiven, redeemed, protected,
saved. Then, uplifted by great impulses of faith, of purity, of

joy, of love and tenderness, we will know that we are no longer ourselves, that another is beginning to live in us, that another has given us his life, and that nothing less than all this love, all this blood, all these sufferings were necessary for us to become, finally, alive.

VII

JESUS CHRIST, WHO SUFFERED AND DIED FOR US

"He who has seen me has seen the Father." Have you meditated on these words in front of Jesus crucified? "The Father who dwells in me does his works." Have you stopped at each station of the way of the cross, looking for the revelation of the Father, the works that the Father teaches to the Son and gives him the capacity to accomplish? "The Son can do nothing of his own accord, but only what he sees the Father doing; for whatever he does, that the Son does likewise. For the Father loves the Son, and shows him all that he himself is doing" (Jn. 5, 19–20). Have we tried to recognize in what the Son does, what the Father shows him?

If the man Christ alone suffers, then say that he alone is Father, that he alone is Love. An impassive Father? Then, you had better stop calling him "Father." An insensitive love? Do not say it is "love."

The revelation of God took place in the greatest suffering. Do not correct the revelation according to the taste of your philosophy. If God manifested himself in that way, it is because there was no means of expressing in our human language, in our human flesh (the Word became flesh), what God is, without expressing suffering.

The conceptions we have of God are, no doubt, all insufficient and must be surpassed. God is Father like us, but also in a completely different way than we. God is Love like us, but also in a completely different way than we. And God is suffering like us, but also in a completely different way than we. Father de Lubac says that the ideas we have of God are like the waves of the sea on which the swimmer relies in order to go beyond them. But the last notions on which we can rely in order to draw nearer to God are precisely those of Father, Love, and Suffering, and he who neglects them loses the support which God wanted to give him. He abandons revelation to go back to theodicy, he leaves the God of Abraham, of Isaac, and of Jacob, to go back to the God of the philosophers and savants. We will never exhaust the understanding of the Incarnation. In choosing poverty, humility, weakness, suffering, God did not appropriate qualities he did not have in order to make himself more attractive! He chose human values which corresponded in a certain way to divine values. When he says that he is Love, and when he says that he is vulnerable, it is not his human nature which he thus characterizes, it is something of his divine nature which he reveals.

Do you know what it is to be a Father?

To be a Father is precisely to suffer; to become a father is to become vulnerable. As long as one is young, one is hard, selfish, protected. No doubt, one has terrible blues, emotions, melancholies, but one holds one's own pretty well, one withdraws easily, one suffers only for oneself. Our compassion for others is gratuitous, generous, superfluous. But when one becomes a father, or a mother, one suddenly sees oneself as vulnerable, in the most sensitive part of one's being; one is completely powerless to defend oneself, one is no longer free, one is tied up. To become a father is to experience an infinite dependency on an infinitely small, frail being, dependent on us and therefore omnipotent over our heart. Oh, we really depend on people who depend on us! The strong person who loves a weak person has put his happiness at his mercy. He depends on him henceforth. He is without any defense against him. To love a person is inevitably to depend on him, to give him power over us. God loved us freely, God gave us power over him. God wanted to have need of us. The passion is the revelation of our terrible power over God. He surrendered himself to us, we had him at our disposal, we did with him what we wanted. On a plaque in Normandy one can read this cruel sentence: "It is always the one who loves the least who is the strongest." It is always he who is least in love who gets his way with the other, who keeps a cool head and stays in control of the situation. God, in regard to us, will always be the weakest, for he loves. God can be denied, forgotten; he cannot deny us, forget us. We can be without God. God cannot be without men. We can stop being sons, he cannot stop being a Father. "Man in revolt against God is like the bird in the storm which dashes itself against the cliff. But God, in his mercy, became flesh so that the violence of the impact might be endured by him and not by us." Thus, God will always be the weakest against us for he loves us. We are of Jacob's race, we are the true Israel, he who fought against the angel all night and who deserved his name: "mighty against God."

When Christ revealed to us the true name of God, he did something greater than Calvary: he surrendered the Father to us. Do you recall the importance of the name for the ancients? A name, for them, evokes so much the thing that is named, that to know the name means to have power over the thing. When Adam takes possession of the animals in paradise, he gives them a name. God confides his mysterious name to the Israelites: "Yahweh," but they designated him by periphrases, so afraid they were of evoking him by naming him. The worst crime of treason consisted in revealing to foreigners, to besiegers, the name of the gods of the city. So great was the strength of the call that the gods, properly called on, obeyed the foreigners.

When Jesus unveiled to us the secret of God, he gave us rights, power, advantage over him. He told us, "Call him: Father." God was then powerless against us. This was the whole mission of Christ. Christ wore himself out to reveal the Father to us, what the Father was like, that the Father himself loved us. And we believed in the Son, in the love, in the goodness of the Son for us. How many Christians imagine that the Son took the initiative of reconciling us with a displeased God: "and to appease his Father's anger." But Christ affirms that he did not come on his own, that he did not come down from heaven to do his own will, but the will of his Father; that he did not take the initiative, but that God so loved the world that he gave his only begotten Son to save the world. Which was harder for the Father: to come in person, or to send his Son? Which was the greater gift?

But, you will say, what can there be in God which corresponds to our suffering? When you tell me that God is a Father, or that he is Love, I can imagine that this concept, properly purified, is not at all contradictory with divine perfection. But the same is not true for suffering. How can we think suffering is compatible with the nature of God?

What idea, precisely, do you have of God? Among all the influences which contribute to our formation, to our evolution, none is more important than the idea we have of God. The whole story of humanity was shattered, deviated, because Adam had a false idea of God. He wanted to become like God. I hope you have never thought that Adam's sin consisted in that. What other ambition can we propose to ourselves? And was it not that, precisely, to which God invited him? Adam was only mistaken in the *means*. He thought that God was an independent, autonomous, sufficient being, and, in order to become like him, he rebelled and disobeyed. But when God revealed himself, when God wanted to show us truly who he was, he revealed himself as love, tenderness, effusion, dependence; God revealed himself as obedient, obedient unto death. God was—what is for man most terrible —God was love. There is nothing man is more afraid of, there is nothing he is more reluctant to do, than to become God. God loves. God is the most audacious being: he has placed all his happiness in his love. He has made all his happiness depend on another. He has placed all his pleasure in another. The Father does not know himself well. He does not love himself. He knows himself, he loves himself only in his Son, his only true image, the work of his love, the radiance of his glory. When he manifests himself, the Father never glorifies himself. He shows us Another in whom he is more himself than in himself, and he says, "This is my beloved Son, listen to him." The Son does not do anything on his own. All that he does manifests the Father. He tells, announces untiringly the glory of the Father, and he goes, joyful, to his passion, to show how the Father taught him to love, to show how a Son loves his Father, how the Father is worthy of being loved. Who sees Christ does not see him but him whom he tries with all his might to reveal and to glorify: the Father.

And the Holy Spirit does not speak on his own. He does not say anything on his own, he says and says again what he has learned from Another with the enthusiasm of admiration and love.

God is humble, for humility is another name for love.

God is poor, too. He is complete self-renunciation. He is all impulse towards another. He has no rest, no satisfaction, no withdrawal into himself. He is perfect ecstasy towards another. He is subsistent relation.

Who would not be afraid of God? Who would not be suspicious of his gifts? God has nothing. He knows only how to love. Then he can only teach how to love, how to give. He lives out of giving. He gives only the capacity of giving. If he taught us how to receive, he would give us nothing of himself. But he wanted so much to communicate himself, to make himself known to us, that he invited us to share his most intimate joy: he gave us the capacity of giving so we might taste the joy of God.

Humility, poverty, suffering are theological virtues; they are the attributes of love. The happiness of God is that of the Beatitudes.

God frightens us, God hurts us. The true answer to the problem of suffering is there. God is for us the most suffering of beings, the most abandoned, the most surrendered, the most committed into the hands of another. He is God at the level of our greatest suffering. Here is the answer to the great modern question: Is God worthy of the suffering of men? Is God unfeeling, smug, sheltered in his heaven, steeped in his happiness? What a poor condition, what a sad idea of God for unhappy men, proud of having suffered and who only feel solidarity and communion with those who suffer like them.

But we Christians deny a solitary and sufficient God, "the eternal Celibate of the worlds," the infinite egoist. No, in the preface of the Mass we pray to the "one God, one Lord, not in the unity of a single person, but in the Trinity of one substance." What a blessing that God is not solitary, what a blessing that he is several! What a joy that he is Love. We believe that God is giving, communication of himself, love. And this is why we believe that in God the worst human distresses find something which welcomes them fraternally, which understands them, which is worthy of them; this is why we believe that our truest communion with God is in suffering, and that it is only through the equivalent of the hardest human renunciation that one can reach the incomprehensible divine felicity. Suffering and happiness are infinitely less contradictory than impassiveness and love. He who imagines God to be merely happy has an untrue idea of him. God's joy emerges from the greatest suffering: he gives his life for what he loves. There is no greater love, there is no greater suffering, there is no greater happiness than to give one's life for those one loves. Such is the sole happiness of God.

"When he was crucified, Christ merely accomplished on this earth, in his distant provinces, amidst the tumult of the elements, what he does unceasingly in his house, in glory and in joy." From all eternity, Christ performs the "Eucharist," gives himself, restores himself, commits himself into the hands of his Father, and there is no act of greater joy. For one hour in the solemn course of centuries, heaven opened up and we witnessed in a flash the eternal happiness of God in his heaven. And we were terrified. We were torn with fear and suffering, we called that crucifixion, bloodiness, passion, and death. In God, love is before all a mutual gift, but in us it means essentially the sacrifice of self-love.

We then understand the cruel deceit of the devil: he made Adam believe that he would become God while remaining himself, that he would be autonomous while setting his face against God. But "the self exists only to be renounced"; to lose it is to save it; to keep it is the worst failure. True autonomy is the possibility of disposing fully of oneself to give oneself to others, and the refusal, the fear of giving means that one is unavailable and therefore lacks true freedom.

Man is a being who does not dare to complete himself. He loves loving, but he is afraid to sacrifice; he loves giving, but he is afraid to lose. He enjoys his independence, he cultivates his autonomous self, but he soon finds it oppressively sterile and monotonous. He wants to take the risk of loving, but he is torn with anxiety when he feels that one cannot at the same time give oneself and keep oneself, do the will of another and continue to live according to one's own. Nearly the equivalent of a molecular rearrangement is necessary in order for man to stop turning around himself and enter into the interests, the views, the life of another. God makes him dizzy by always proposing a game of "he who wins, loses." It is through death that the redemption is accomplished, it is through suffering that one finds happiness.

God would not be Love if he did not live that constantly. Still today the progress of grace in our souls faithfully carries on the mission of Jesus among his contemporaries. It is sensitive to our welcome and vulnerable to our denials. Like Jesus, grace penetrates, invades, uplifts those who open themselves to it. And it complains, it weeps, it becomes silent little by little before those who abandon it. To each of us Jesus risen appears as to St. Paul: "I am Jesus whom you are persecuting." To each of us Jesus glorified, deserted like a poor man, complains, "Here I am at the door and I knock. He who will open to me, I will enter his home and eat with him the evening meal."

Do not grieve the Holy Spirit, St. Paul says.

Love wanted to be vulnerable, God wanted to love us to the point of suffering from it.

This is what made St. Paul the most indignant in the Jewish heresy which nascent Christianity seemed to be: a God-man, humiliated, feeling! He, of whom one could not make a hewed image through respect for his transcendence, represented like an executed prisoner!

And yet this is what was taught to him from his first revelation on. In a flash, on the road to Damascus, Saul learned the whole Christian religion: "Saul, Saul, why do you persecute me?" He learned that Jesus knew him, Saul himself, loved him, Saul himself, to the point of suffering, of giving him the power of crucifying him again.

"I am Jesus whom you are persecuting." The whole doctrine, the whole destiny of Paul burst from this experience: the incorporation of Christians into Christ, not only of Christian martyrs, but even of the least "man of the Church," like the fearful and recalcitrant Ananias; and above all the incredibly generous love of Christ for us. If Jesus loved us in this way, if God had given us such power over him that we were capable of persecuting him, torturing him, putting him to death, then Paul's career was fixed, his future was open, he knew what was going to fill his life; all this power he had over God, and which until then he had used to make him suffer, he was going henceforth to use to honor and serve him. Since Christ had given himself to Paul to this point, Paul would give himself to Christ. And to atone for his previous persecutions, Paul would hasten the glorious Advent by gathering, creating, edifying for him this Body which was at once that of God and ours, and which Christ had entrusted to him.

VIII

MEDITATIONS

You only become the saint you do not want to become

You will never become a saint in the way you imagine or hope. One can become a saint only by accepting a will other than one's own. I often imagine the story of an old, worn man, of an elderly and disappointed woman, whose every good desire has run aground, whom God has constantly hindered in their most generous plans.

Their vocation, put to the test, has been denied; their attempts at the apostolate have failed for miserable reasons of money or machination, their marriage is sterile or their children are dead, their life is useless.

They grow old anxious and lonely, surrounded by ruins.

But when, sometimes, on their knees, in a long, mute prayer, they dare to question the impenetrable Providence who has conducted their lives, when they reach out their empty hands towards God, when they offer him their wasted existence, their hearts which have beaten so little, it comes about that they receive a strangely comforting answer. They sometimes come to understand, in a disarming light, that everything is quite as he wanted it, that their own will would have led them to human results, but that God preferred to lead them to him, that he reserved them entirely for himself, so that the witness they bear to him is pure.

"Yes, I have shattered your projects, I have annihilated your pride. Nobody needs you, you live without self-contentment, you are before me like a lamp which shines for the satisfaction of nobody, —you are 'without any purpose.' But you are my love and my glory, I placed my delight in you, you are the portion reserved to me, so well preserved that you are wanted by nobody else, and that you do not even think of being useful, you are my purest reflection because you have become the saints you did not want to become."

Our life is a prayer which is heard

Our prayer is always heard, but not at the time or in the way we had imagined.

We think we have not been heard, we forget our prayers and we continue on our way, resigned to the refusal of God.

But God hears each prayer. God hears each prayer for the infallible reason that it is he who has inspired it.

It is he who wants to give, and we who are not ready to receive, with our attachments to the very evil we want him to deliver us from, with our fear of the grace we think we implore.

It is he who keeps our prayers in his heart, to answer them as soon as we are mature enough not to oppose them any longer.

We are not faithful, but God is faithful.

We are not persevering, but God is persevering.

He keeps in us all that we promised him. He who has offered himself, is taken; he who has asked, receives; to him who has knocked, the door is opened!

Try it: as soon as you have asked to suffer, you will begin to suffer. And it is very likely that you will be so surprised at such promptness that you will hesitate to recognize in it the effect of your prayer.

Often, before people overburdened by trials, failure, mourning, illness, separation, I have been led to ask them a question through listening to them, looking at them, hearing them: "But haven't you ever offered that? Haven't you ever said to God that you would accept that? Haven't you ever prayed for that?"

Then, sometimes, they are struck, they meditate and remember. In enlightened and fervent moments, they have said that to God, they have offered him everything; they have accepted and asked for the cross. They recall an old forgotten prayer, which they did not think so sincere—and so well heard.

Men say terrible things: "I offer myself to you, I give you everything. Take me, Father, thy kingdom come," and above all: "thy will be done."

Then they go off leaving this ineffective aspiration—or so they believe—behind.

But God has gathered it in, he preserves it and will present it to you in due time.

The life of a priest is spent in making men understand God's plan for their life, the faithfulness with which he loves them, calls them, and guides them.

Our obscure and tormented life will be enlightened, perhaps, if we remember an old forgotten prayer which God has gathered in.

God's way of speaking

A remarkable book has this romantic title: God Will Speak This Evening. The title is false, but it expresses a very widespread error: for God will not speak to us one evening; God speaks to us all the time. He has always spoken to us in his language, in the severe and simple language of our daily existence. We do not hear him because we would like him to speak in ours, in our language of happiness such as we imagine it, through poor and silly satisfactions of feeling, self-love, or even comfort, the only messages that we have decided to recognize as his.

But God speaks to us with perseverance in his language. God speaks to us in this language, unknown to us and which we are reluctant to learn, of acceptance, of sacrifice, or renunciation, the language of a prodigiously far-reaching, uncon-

ceivably audacious, incredibly generous plan through which
he wants to save us, us and the world. God speaks to us
unceasingly through the events of our life, through his
obstinacy in thwarting our petty human plans, through his
punctuality in disappointing our projects and our attempts to
escape, through the perpetual failure of all our calculations
to manage to do without him. And, little by little, he tames
us, he familiarizes us. One day, when we are confined to our
bed, checkmated by a failure, isolated by a misfortune, annihilated by the feeling of our powerlessness, one day, he
resigns us to listen to his language, to admit his presence, to
acknowledge his will.

And we know then that he was speaking to us all the time.

The right cross

We all know that a Christian must bear the cross. We are all
disposed, theoretically, to accept one. But have you noticed
that it is never the right cross which comes to us? The cross
we bear (our health, our face, our embarrassment, our wife,
our husband, our mother, our child) always seems to us unbearable, petty, humiliating, harmful. It is always precisely
what should not have become our lot, precisely what we cannot accept for all kinds of obvious reasons which we are always
harping on. All the other crosses seem preferable to us, that of
our neighbor, the previous one—that which we have imagined.
Ours is hateful, it destroys us, it hurts us—imagine, it em-
bitters us, and we have a grudge against ourselves and
against everybody. We desperately call for another, for a cross
which "fits in," a bearable, spiritual, elevating cross, beneficial
to us and to others.

But alas, we must come to recognize that if the cross suited
us, it would no longer be a cross; that if we refuse those which
hurt, we refuse any cross; and that the cross which God par-
cels out to us must necessarily always be humiliating and painful, paralyzing and difficult, and must hurt us at the spot
where we are the most defenseless.

Mortification

We must know how to detach ourselves even from suffering. We must learn to be happy even when we are unhappy. We must, in a word, work loose from ourselves. A Father of the Church used to say to himself, "There is only one way of being cured of sadness, and that is to dislike being sad." It is hard to believe this when we are suffering. As if we had chosen to be hurt! Of course not, but what is terrible is that we often choose to keep on suffering, to fan the flames of our pain, to inflame our wounds, to find our only comfort in our very discomfort. For if we keep our pain, then we also keep our right to complain, our right to withdraw into our shell, our right to hurt others and to kill their joy. And when there is no joy in the world any longer, then we will be confirmed in our pain. We have, in the meantime, only one stone to rest our head on, and it is called despair. This hard pillow will give us long service.

Indeed, nothing would be harder than to stop being happy. There is no worse detachment than joy.

Simon of Cyrene

He is one of those who have to be grabbed and forced to bear the cross. Nothing was more distasteful to him. He thought his day finished. He was expected, he was needed somewhere else. But they seized him, and covering him with insults, constrained him to bear the cross. Simon was revolted by the injustice, indignant that such a bad job fell upon him. He was not even alone: he had to walk second, in an obliged association with an insulted and staggering wretch.

Then they started on their way. The other in front, Simon behind. And Simon learned how to walk slowly, to stop, to start again at the will of Another, to follow in his footsteps, and conform his will to Another's will. Little by little, his attention turned towards this man before him who dragged himself along without saying a word, towards this patient companion who did not look back and whose silence in the end impressed him. He learned to observe this other man, his patience which nothing tired, his prodigious capacity of suffering, his infinite gentleness in consoling those who were weeping, in rewarding those who were helping him, in forgiving those who were insulting him. He felt the radiance of his strength and his gentleness surrounding him and penetrating him, and he longed to draw nearer to him. Simon was changing, Simon had never learned so much. Simon was learning Jesus under the cross. And whereas in the beginning he only saw the cross—hateful and repugnant—in the end he saw only Jesus.

He had struggled so much, he had protested so much against this cross and now he would not want to be elsewhere for anything in the world, he was becoming attached, he was staying there voluntarily, he was passionately kissing the cross which had been imposed upon him.

The Good Thief

They both began by insulting him.

Was it rage at seeing this "innocent" prey and forgive in the midst of their cries of revolt? Shame at being mingled with this weak character? Obscure jealousy of something lacking in them? Despair of one who, treed on his wood, is mad at everybody because he can no longer expect anything from anybody?

For it is certainly not easier to bear a pain because one "had it coming"!

If one pays one's "due," one should at least have the right to curse the process-server, the law court, the witnesses, the spectators, all those who make one pay.

If God is but just, if he but knows this job of tradesman and judge: to make one pay the price, —I am "quits" with him as soon as he enforces on me his rates and his constraints.

Only the innocent can guess that there is a gratuitousness,

a generosity proposed to his suffering which are the secret of another world, of another Being. Only the innocent is able not to be ashamed of suffering, not to be denounced, accused, betrayed by his suffering.

But doesn't any profound suffering strike in addition the part of innocence which remains in us?

Isn't there in each guilty person who is punished, as much as he may be absorbed in his suffering, something which, precisely through this excess of misfortune and solitude, becomes free to offer and to love?

One of them watched Jesus better, saw him better than the other. And the availability and freshness which is in him awakens, is moved in watching how Jesus suffers, and how he loves in suffering. (How many people will become converted, like him, by watching us suffer? By seeing Jesus who suffers in us?)

And they will learn like him that deserved sufferings can nonetheless call back, assimilate, incorporate one into Christ.

That suffering is a kind of sacrament, for him who receives it without hatred.

That all suffering can be useful, even the just punishments for shameful crimes. That the imposed and just suffering can unite with the offering of free and undeserved sufferings.

That God is of another order than that of exact retribution.

And that in only one wing-stroke, he lifts us up with him, infinitely beyond all this bargaining:

"Truly, I say to you, today you will be with me in paradise!"

God has taken from me . . .

No, God is not the one who takes. He is the Father, he gives. He loves us first. He is source of life and of joy. He enjoys gratifying us with his gifts. He only reveals himself to us through his blessings, and his glory is that we find his work good.

He likes only to give. But by dint of gifts, he teaches us

how to give. If God had done nothing but give, he would have given nothing of himself. God is gift, God is love. He does not reveal himself to him who only knows how to receive. But to him whom he cherishes most, to him to whom he wants to communicate himself completely, he gives the capacity of becoming a father, he gives the capacity of being gift in his turn. He wanted so much to communicate himself, to make himself known, that he invited us to share his most intimate joy: he gave us the taste for giving in order that we might know the taste of the joy of God.

If God calls us to sacrifice, let us not force ourselves, let us not cut by ourselves the ties which hurt us so much. Let us open ourselves to God, let us let God fill us, let us let God become God in us. Let us remain before him in silence until, by dint of gift and love, he uplifts us to give and love in our turn.

Creature

There is no worse suffering than to be a creature. We are like a word which one never finishes pronouncing, eternally suspended and uncertain about its own meaning. A word which does not hear the voice which pronounces it. A word which must be content to let itself be pronounced.

Or else we are like rough-casts which have escaped from the hands of our modeller.

We are sick and tired of being hurt, of blows, scrapings, cuttings, remodellings. But when we stop in our furious flight, we find ourselves miserable, terribly insufficient, incapable of expressing ourselves and of finding our bearings, and we cry with anger and indignation against him who is responsible for it.

There is no rest, for a creature, except in the hands of his creator. He alone can complete it, free it from its anxiety and its distress. But the place of its completion is also the place of its pain, the place where God is at work on it. There is no peace for us except in relying on the place where we are hurt.

Hope

God does not protect us against catastrophes. He is neither a lightning-rod nor a breakwater. But he comes to our aid in catastrophes. It is in the very midst of the tempest and the misfortune that a wonderful zone of peace, serenity, and joy bursts in us, if we dwell in his grace. God does not help us before we have helped ourselves. God does not relieve us before we have exhausted our own strength.

But when we are at the end of our resources, when everything is going the worst, when everything is taking place as if he did not exist or could not do anything, at this moment he manifests himself, and we begin to know that he has been there all along.

We should not "count on" God. He is supremely free and unforeseeable. But we should hope in him against all hope.

It is when you are the most unhappy that you will find yourselves the most happy. Never will you have known greater peace, simplification, and fervor than when you are completely unhappy. The weight of your unhappiness crushes you, but against God, to the point of not leaving any space between him and you. Your powerlessness, your total misery will make your liberation. You will learn then that existence is a gratuitous gift and not an anxious personal industry. And the intensity of the hope which will bloom so simply in your heart will reveal to you the violence with which you had repressed it until then.

You will know that nothing was more natural to you than to entrust yourself, whereas you were trying to use even your first move of confidence towards God in order not to entrust yourself truly to him, but to try to make him enter into your plans, like a pawn on your chess-board. It is only when you accepted to be a pawn in his hand and in his plan, that you liberated your hope and his action.

Knock . . .

Father, teach me to knock.

I am closed in upon myself, I am on the wrong side of the door. I faintly remember that there is another side, but I am not capable of going there, and I am not even sure I want to.

It is so much easier to stay on this side.

Indeed, I am willing to knock on this door and to strike it, I am willing to hurl myself against it, to hurt myself on it. But I have no hope that the door will open, and I do not even desire it.

It is difficult to learn to knock well, Lord. To knock means to appeal to someone else, it means to wait, to correspond. Lord, it is all that I do not know how to do!

Instead of thinking mournfully of myself, instead of complaining, and wantonly making myself unhappy, I would have to think of another, to think that there exists another Being whom I could address, who is waiting, who is listening and hoping, on his part, for the sign of my confidence and the appeal of my friendship.

Lord, I know, in a certain way, it is true, the door is already open. When I will turn back to make the gesture, when, tears in my eyes, humble, already appeased, I will turn in order to knock timidly at the door, moderating my gesture in order to intensify my faith and not to jar on the attentive ear which is listening, I will find the door open, I will push it with one finger, and I will still hold myself back from opening it too quickly, in order to prepare a little for the meeting with him who is much more anxious to open than I to enter. I will know then that I am not ready, and that the gift I claim, I hate, I still refuse at the moment when I reproach you for not giving it to me.

Lord, teach us to knock, to understand that it is not up to us to teach you to open. We are the ones who shut the doors, Lord. We shut ourselves behind so many doors, we become frantic in the place where we have fled. Teach us to calm ourselves, to remain tranquil a while, to breathe, to listen, to awaken from our bad nightmares, in your arms.

Lord, one knocks only because you give the capacity of knocking.

Lord, isn't it rather you who knock, and I who do not want to open?

Burden

In spite of appearances we all bear the same burden: I mean, one that is unbearable.

As long as one is young, one imagines that there are happy, innocent, protected beings. And one is scandalized by the odious inequality of human destinies. Rich people have everything at their disposal, even culture, even education, even religious lights and assurances. So many miserable people do not know anything about what justifies their existence; they have no leisure to wonder about it; they endure life, and then they are thrown out of it.

But in advancing in age, in approaching men, in entering into their intimacy, in receiving their confidences, you will come to understand that they are all guilty and that they are all unhappy.

Each man bears a burden exactly like that of all others in this: it is just beyond his strength! The equality of men is there. There is a prodigious fraternity in the human condition: everybody gasps under a weight which he is incapable of bearing. Each one experiences a fundamental powerlessness. Each one measures his nothingness. Each one learns, through his burden, what is that of all the others.

The mature man knows that the world is beautiful, the universe rich, existence varied and savory, and, at the same time, that life is impossible, that it has always been so, that it will always be so, and that one must not be merely man in order to face it.

Faith is this complement of reasons and forces without which our scale is for ever unbalanced.

It does not hurt so much to be hurt . . .

What is unbearable is not to suffer but to be afraid of suffering. To endure a precise pain, a definite loss, a hunger for something one knows—this it is possible to bear. One can live with this pain. But in fear there is all the suffering of the world: to dread suffering is to suffer an infinite pain since one supposes it unbearable; it is to revolt against the universe, to lose one's place and one's rights in it, to become vulnerable over the whole extent of one's being.

Paetus's wife taught him this when, compelled with her husband to commit suicide at the command of the Emperor (tyrants of that time had so well perfected their methods that they saved the expense of executioners), she snatched out of his hands the dagger which he hesitatingly held, and plunged it into her breast, saying, *"Paete, non dolet."* It does not hurt so much to be hurt.

One of my friends, rejected by his fiancée, told me, "As long as I try to act as if I were not suffering, as long as I flirt with other girls, as long as I try not to think of her, I am like a madman, I have a horrible inner emptiness, I do not dare to stop: each second the sorrow can rush upon me and annihilate me. But if I think deeply, if I become aware again of what I have lost, if I accept being deprived of it for ever, then I experience a strong, confident peace of mind which I never thought possible. It is only in my suffering that I find support and rest."

Loving your pain

You would not like, you say, loving your pain? . . . Well, I would! It is a shame the way we treat it. There is nothing in us which is more mistreated, more scoffed at. In the family of our feelings, it is the outcast. If it is at all possible, we ignore it, we tuck it in the farthest corner of our being. Sometimes we even succeed in banishing it to our subconscious.

You can see it crouched there, distended in its grief. But it is very alive, like all the other feelings, eager to live like the others, ready to rise up at the merest opportunity. And that means, in the long run, that it is ready for any excess . . .

The majority of people recognize the existence of pain, they "bear" it, and the best even accept it, —but never at once. How many struggles, discussions, tribulations are necessary before we even "accept" our pain! And even then, we do not accept it as pain. We have to rename it. We have to call it "renunciation" or "sacrifice," in order to dull the razor edge of suffering. We accept pain, but only if we can disguise it.

Pain, believe me, does not like this kind of treatment. Like a rebuffed, frustrated, ignored child, it has to attract attention to itself, all of the time. It will groan, complain, cry, yell, scream, pout, do anything that is necessary in order to take our attention away from our other feelings. Pain wants to occupy all of our being, and this merely because we do not give it its place among the others, merely because we dare not look into its face, give it a chance to live peacefully within us.

Of course, pain is violent, overflowing. Often it comes to you suddenly, without your being prepared, and you do not know that it must be welcomed. Then it forces everything, invades everything, makes you deaf to everything but its cries. Do not be afraid, be patient, do not take pleasure in it, but smile on it, let it shout like mad, pray. . . . There will come a time when it will be tired, when its outcries will decrease, when it will find its place in you, when it will feel not only accepted but loved—yes, loved—for, just as with men, that is the only thing which appeases it.

Besides, why would we not really love it? Of course, it hurts. . . . The lancet of the surgeon cutting our flesh hurts too in order to cure us. Pain . . . pain does much more than to cure us of ourselves, it detaches us from ourselves, it puts us on our knees, it makes us abandon everything to the Father because we feel that alone we are incapable of bearing it and of receiving it "well." It makes us enter at once into the great brotherhood of mankind, where those who are waiting for us and will turn their faces towards us, will read in our eyes what we have made of it. We will see faces revolted, crushed, desperate, or merely suffering, hardened into indifference because they did not know how to love pain. Which message will we bring to them, *you and I,* if we don't love it? How will they know that there is a way of being happy, abandoned, joyous, confident, with a burning pain in a corner of our being, that this pain has in us the place which it deserves, that it is necessary to us and that we love it so well that it does not even think of trespassing on its neighbors, that it lets them live too: faith, wonder, love, adoration, thanksgiving, trust, peace, serenity, and all the others which crowd around us to fill us with courage, hope, and love so that we may continue to advance.

I thought I had said the essential, but, as I grow older, I perceive that I must absolutely add something. It is this: that we must know that although it has its place in us, there will still be some days when pain will invade us completely; just as each child, in a large family, comes in turn entirely to preoccupy his parents when he goes through a crisis. At this moment, everything is for him, he occupies every fibre of their being, and it is his right. When these days come, love your pain more than ever, with great patience, never forgetting that if it may preoccupy and invade you for a while, other children are still there who need your time and your love, and who are waiting to take up your full attention in their turn.

The sacrifice of being happy

The great virtue to practice during the Easter season is joy. At any moment, the Church interrupts her prayer during Mass or during the service to utter cries of jubilation, endless alleluias.

And Jesus warns us that it is this joy which will distinguish us from the "world." "Yet a little while and the world will see me no more," he said shortly before his passion, "but you will see me . . . and I will see you again and your hearts will rejoice, and no one will take your joy from you."

Now, it is a strange thing: we are not in harmony with this joy. We are better disposed to be sorrowful with Christ than to rejoice; we more easily share his sufferings than his joy.

The greatest sacrifice, the costliest renunciation which we should offer to God, is to be happy.

Indeed, in this time of pessimism, of international anxiety, of trouble and doubt, the duty of being happy should be greatly emphasized.

We are like St. Thomas. You know that the Gospel relates only two traits of his character, and these seem to be, at first sight, contrary to one another. When Jesus is going to raise Lazarus, the frightened disciples say to him, "Rabbi, the Jews were but now seeking to stone you, and you are going there again?" (Jn. 11, 8). Jesus tells them to be confident and that nothing harmful can happen to them as long as they walk with him. And Thomas says to the others, "Let us also go, that we may die with him!" Which is not a word of faith, not even of genuine generosity, but the sign of a bitter and strong pessimism, like that which will later on make him reject so forcibly the Resurrection.

Well, we are like him, pessimists, maybe courageous pessimists in that we do not refuse suffering, but pessimists who do not want, at any price, to believe in happiness. During Lent, for example, we have perhaps mortified ourselves, or, at least, we have thought of doing so. We have attended Lenten services, and who has not felt that Good Friday was a day different from all the others?

But since Easter, since the resurrection, our religious life is on vacation, we have finished our liturgical year with the relief, but also the separation, of Holy Saturday. We no longer see our role.

And yet, there is something so selfish, so hard in refusing to share the joy of a friend and in accepting only his sufferings, in leaving him at the very moment when we could give him the greatest joy, that of allowing him to do us good. But the true explanation of this attitude of ours is a profounder one. We are sorrowful, we mortify ourselves with our Lord more willingly than we rejoice over his resurrection because, in suffering, we seek ourselves, we find ourselves easily. Our naturally pessimistic temperament is in harmony with these tragic events, and we always have good reasons to be sad "on our own account" which allow us to pity ourselves while looking as if we pitied him.

But to share the joy of another, this is the occasion and the sign of a genuine attachment and disinterestedness, since it is a joy in which there is nothing of us, where we find ourselves so little.

After Lent, there still remains the greatest mortification, the greatest renunciation, that which was prepared by all the others and which will prove their sincerity: we must make to God the sacrifice of being happy. We must give God this joy, this reward: to see us happy. Tell him that after all that he did and suffered for us, we cannot really live on anything else than the joy of his love, we are so much tied and united to him, we live so much on him that, when we think it over, we no longer find anything alive in us but his joy.

Happiness

Happiness is like a wake, it faithfully follows him who does not pursue it. If one stops to contemplate it, to grasp it, to make sure of it, it vanishes at once. We must aim at truth, sacrifice, duty, or death in order to realize suddenly that we are happy. From the moment we have renounced, we discover that we have only sacrificed our chains and that we have so painfully immolated our torments.

Happiness has something profoundly painful and heavy about it. It involves accepting to plunge again into our condition, out of which we are trying to escape. Like the ploughshare, we have to be unceasingly dug profoundly into full earth, by a merciless hand, in order to find, in darkness and effort, our usefulness and value.

Happiness is like a fire, it is impossible to create one which will be only good for our personal use. We have to produce enough heat to warm up a world before being able, like the last of our poor, to come and sit down by the fire we have offered to the others.

You must be absolutely happy, at once, under pain of never becoming so. What you miss cannot deprive you of happiness. You will always miss something. If you cannot be happy without it, you will never be so. You must give happiness credit. You must be happy in advance, you must trust in being happy, you must be happy even when you are unhappy.

Ordinarily, we do not know how to go about being happy, we are happy without knowing it, or without wanting to know it, awkwardly, resentfully, tepidly. A moment of forgetfulness, of innocence or faith, and we will find ourselves reconciled with life, we will find it good, just, gratuitous. As soon as we stop blaming life for what it has not given to us, we will see that it was only our lack of confidence which made life seem in need of justification.

OTHER IMAGE BOOKS

OTHER IMAGE BOOKS

OTHER IMAGE BOOKS

OTHER IMAGE BOOKS

OTHER IMAGE BOOKS

OTHER IMAGE BOOKS